CO-DEPENDENCE

CO-DEPENDENCE

Misunderstood—Mistreated

ANNE WILSON SCHAEF

HarperSanFrancisco

A Division of HarperCollins*Publishers*

CO-DEPENDENCE: *Misunderstood—Mistreated*. Copyright © 1986 by Anne Wilson Schaef. Printed in the United States of America. No part of this book may be used or reproduced in any manner whatsoever without written permission except in the case of brief quotations embodied in critical articles and reviews. For information address HarperCollins Publishers, 10 East 53rd Street, New York, NY 10022.

FIRST EDITION

Library of Congress Cataloging-in-Publication Data
Schaef, Anne Wilson.
    Co-dependence : misunderstood—mistreated / Anne Wilson
Schaef. — 1st ed.
      p.   cm.
    Includes bibliographical references.
    ISBN 0–86683–486–9 (pbk. : alk. paper)
    1. Co-dependence (Psychology) I. Title.
RC569.5.C63S33 1992
616.86—dc20   90–56441
                                          CIP

91 92 93 94 95 M-V 10 9 8 7 6 5 4 3 2 1

This edition is printed on acid-free paper that meets the American National Standards Institute Z39.48 Standard.

Contents

To all those persons who are suffering from this previously unnamed disease and who have not known that they have a disease that can be treated and from which they can recover.

To those courageous enough to acknowledge having this disease and be willing to teach us about it.

To those professionals who have stretched their conceptual boundaries to name and begin to treat this insidious and pervasive disease.

To all of us who seek recovery and are joyfully recovering.

Acknowledgments

First and foremost, I want to acknowledge the members of my family, who continue to say, "Go for it, Mom." I also want to acknowledge my clients, the participants at my workshops, my trainees, and myself for providing many opportunities to experience firsthand the disease of co-dependence. Not only have we watched, laughed with, and learned from each other, we have generated ideas together. My trainees have spent hours listening to my theories, questioning me, and putting me on the spot until I could articulate these theories more clearly.

I want to thank Vickie, Diane, and the staff aboard the Royal Viking Sea for inventing imaginative and creative ways to get this book written in the United States, on the Atlantic Ocean, and in Europe.

Lastly, I want to thank the people at Winston Press for their willingness to push their publishing schedule and get this book into print.

CO-DEPENDENCE

Introduction to the New Edition

Has it only been six years since I first penned an introduction to my book *Co-Dependence: Misunderstood—Mistreated,* then stating that I wanted to get my ideas about this new concept in on the ground floor? Astonishingly, the concept and most of the ideas in this book seem as relevant today as they did when the book was first written. Certainly, the title is perhaps even more to the point than it was six years ago.

When we talked about a new introduction, the publisher asked me to try to respond to some of the controversy that is raging about the concept of co-dependency. I personally find this focus very difficult because I experience the issues raised by critics as so insane that it almost requires a plunge into the addictive process to even try to respond to them.

For example, a critic was recently on a national talk show promoting his book, which viciously attacks the concept of co-dependence. (I refuse to give his name or the title of the book because I do not want to support or promote him or his book in any way!) He had two main criticisms that he repeated over and over, refusing to listen to any input from the audience or anyone else. The first was, "People are making *money* off of co-dependence!!" . . . Now that's an interesting critique! Isn't he making money promoting his book attacking co-dependence? Isn't that why he was on the show, to sell his books? And, as a therapist, doesn't his very livelihood depend upon making money off of other people's problems? Yet, the implication is that there is something inherently wrong (or evil, perhaps) in making money off of a concept that helps people heal. I find this kind of thinking confusing.

His other frequently repeated statement was, "The *experts* are telling people that they are addicts and co-dependents." Again, another strange statement coming from someone who considers himself an expert and gets paid for diagnosing and treating people from his perspective. Ironically, the whole interest in co-dependence has grown in a grass roots way by people naming and claiming this "disease" for themselves and seeking recovery in a way that does not include the expert-authority model. Indeed, most of the writers in the field are writing from the perspective of their own struggles with this addictive process and are only sharing their "experience, strength, and hope." How does individual sharing get twisted into "experts," and then how does the use of "experts" become "bad" when he, himself, comes from a paradigm that believes in and supports experts, himself being one? This kind of thinking always confuses me.

I also noticed that this particular "expert against experts" was incapable of hearing person after person in the audience refute his hypothesis. Again and again they stated that "no one had told them that they were addicts or co-dependents." They had discovered that for themselves.

In these interactions, I saw another characteristic that I have come to recognize in opponents of the concept of co-dependence: the inability to listen, explore, discuss, or be open to new information. The basic style seems to be "don't confuse me with the facts and, *most of all,* don't confuse me with your experience or your truth." What is the *real* issue? I continue to wonder.

Some time ago, I thought I would write an article responding to some of the almost violent articles that have come out against addiction, co-dependence, and recovery. Here are some of the ideas I developed . . .

There is a trend against a trend. What is this about? Seemingly coming from a place of ignorance and non-participatory judgmentalism, it is now chic to criticize how chic it has become to participate in twelve step groups.

Under the guise of a critical, objective, scientific mind set, writers such as Stanton Peele (*The Diseasing of America*) lash out with pseudo-rational emotionalism. There's nothing wrong with emotionalism. It is only when it hides under the guise of rationalism and objective science that it becomes frightening and dangerous. Such critics seem to forget that the very basis of science is open-mindedness and the ability to explore new ideas and new concepts from a position of clarity (sobriety?) within oneself.

Why, might I ask, are these sophisticated, critical thinkers not being open to the exploration of the *truths* that exist in the new awareness about addiction and co-dependence? In recovering circles, the kind of thinking that we see in many of these articles would be nailed as "stinkin' thinkin'" (confused reasoning characteristic of the addictive process), and people would be encouraged to do their own work and get clear before they dumped their own issues on others.

Unfortunately, this degree of clarity does not seem to be a criteria applied in the publication decisions of magazines such as the *New York Times Book Review, Family Circle, Playboy,* and others. I have noticed a decided bias in publishing these volatile, emotional, often nasty attacks on the concepts of addiction and co-dependence while giving no space or credence to the concepts themselves. I do know that as I have tried to read some of this material, I have felt covered over with a slimy goo, and that in trying to respond, I am forced to enter into a system that I perceive as unhealthy and that I do not like.

Another issue that gives me great concern is the joining of feminists and mental health professionals in this attack. At first glance, these two seem to be strange "bedgals" indeed. Yet, I have experienced this teaming up to be common and frequent. I have no idea what has happened to the feminism of the sixties and seventies that was suspicious of psychotherapy and its power differential and attempts to keep women in a patriarchal system. I see many women who call themselves feminists aligning themselves with a mental health approach and a way of thinking that solidly locks them into the very patriarchy they try to avoid. I know that sometimes my need to understand this phenomenon often interferes with my acceptance of its truth for some people.

What I do know is that my entry to recovery was through the door of co-dependence and that there is no discrepancy whatsoever between recovery from addictions and feminism for me. The two go hand-in-hand and are mutually supportive. What I know is that it is a *relief* to see this connection. I have a disease process that I learned in the society. I can recover and no longer play the role of victim that the mental health system would impose upon me. In my recovery, I do not have to accept either end of the victim/perpetrator dualism, and neither do I have to orient myself to that dualism. I have come to know that as I free myself from my addictions, I also free myself from a mechanistic, scientific worldview that requires sexism, racism, homophobia, and ageism in all their subtle forms.

My recovery has also allowed me to understand with all my being a scientific and spiritual worldview that is much more in keeping with my knowledge as a woman. Recovery has taught me the wonders of full participation in my life the way I define it.

And, yet, co-dependence was only a door for me. As I progressed in my recovery, I began to see that even though the concept of co-dependence offered me a "way" into recovery, after I had progressed in my recovery it became a roadblock. I could see that I was using the "co" term in two destructive ways to block my further progress: (1) I was using it to feed my one-ups-womanship to feel just a little superior to "those addicts"; and (2) I was continuing to use it to externally referent, be a victim, and not claim my own life. So, I had to face yet another shift. I had to admit I was an addict . . . a relationship *addict* . . . just like any other addict. And then my recovery took off.

So, I believe that the term co-dependence has been a useful door for many who decide to step upon the road to recovery, *and* I believe that in all recovery we need to move on. The recovery movement needs to move on and we as individuals need to move on. Nothing that is alive is static. Stasis belongs to a scientific worldview that is entropic and devouring itself.

This book continues to be an important door. Let's use it that way.

*We are beginning to recognize that
co-dependence is a disease in its own right.*

chapter one

The History and
Development of the
Concept of Co-Dependence

Since the concept of co-dependence has evolved so recently,
we have not yet seen an integrative theory developed about
it. Co-dependence has the beauty of being a "grass-roots"
idea. That is to say, people who admit to having the disease
themselves and are in the process of recovering from it are
developing theories about co-dependence, not professionals
who have only a "left-brain" interest in the disease. The
awareness of the dynamics of co-dependence comes directly
out of the struggle, the pain, and the elation of working
through an illness and beginning to know that there is
another way to live and be with others.

This process of understanding and evolving a theory
about a disease from within is not foreign to the chemical
dependency (or CD) field. In the CD field, the persons
most trusted are those who can honestly say, "I know how
you feel"—those who, themselves, are struggling (and have
struggled) internally with the ravages of alcoholism and admit
it. In the field of mental health, on the other hand, practitioners generally do not admit to having *any* problems and

are seen as less effective if they *have* to admit to some of the problems with which they work.

At this point in its development, co-dependence is understood and used almost exclusively within the field of chemical dependency. Most professionals and lay people who are not somehow involved in the CD field know little or nothing about this disease and its treatment. I firmly believe, in fact—as many others have suggested (among them, Sharon Wegscheider-Cruse, Jael Greenleaf, Charles Whitfield, to name a few)—that most mental health professionals are untreated co-dependents who are actively practicing their disease in their work in a way that helps neither them nor their clients. The ignorance of the mental health profession about this disease has resulted in costly, long-range, and ineffective treatment for co-dependents. It has, however, kept the professional's pockets lined, and it has probably served to perpetuate her or his own co-dependence.

The Chemical Dependency Field

As I understand the development of the concept of co-dependence within the CD field, it has been employed in relation to the treatment of the alcoholic. We all know that prior to the development of the disease concept of alcoholism, the alcoholic was considered a bad, weak person who just had no willpower. Alcoholism was a disease from which the individual recovered in isolation from the family and usually only with the support of other "drunks." As Virginia Satir developed her concepts of family therapy, Vernon Johnson, Sharon Wegscheider-Cruse, and others began to look at alcoholism as a family disease, and the entire field opened itself to the awareness that the alcoholic was not the only person affected by the disease. It became clear, in fact, that the entire family was affected and that each member played a role in helping the disease perpetuate itself.

Since many of the initial contributions in the CD area came from people who were themselves recovering alcoholics, the emphasis in treatment continued to be on the recovery of the alcoholic and on describing elements that would impede that recovery. It was accurately believed that alcoholics would have less chance of staying sober if they returned to untreated families, which would enable them to drink by making excuses for them and by otherwise continuing to practice their own co-dependence. Hence, CD counselors began working with families to serve the recovery of the alcoholic. Since the entire family had revolved around the alcoholic and the disease, it was not difficult to convince the family to continue focusing upon the alcoholic. So the family members dutifully learned about the disease of alcoholism and were told that they were sick. Exactly how they were sick and how they were to recover remained a mystery.

I want to emphasize here how much, historically, the initial treatment of the family focused all of its energies on the alcoholic. The term *enabler,* for instance, which is used in chemical dependency circles to describe the person—usually the spouse—who subtly helps support the drinking, is obviously oriented toward the alcoholic. The focus in working with the enabler was on helping her or him learn not to help perpetuate the disease in the alcoholic; little was done to help the enabler recover from her or his disease. Those providing this focus were usually recovering alcoholics, who had a vested personal interest in alcoholism per se.

There then was a time when the terms *enabler* and *co-dependent* were used almost interchangeably. The enabler/co-dependent was usually the spouse of the chemically dependent person, and there was tacit recognition that other members of the family were also co-dependents. However, the focus of treatment remained primarily on the alcoholic, on the spouse secondarily, and on the children least of all, a procedure that simply replicated the experience of the sick family itself. Family members were often described as co-dependent *to* the alcoholic, and their disease was not understood as a disease process in its own right. Even though Al-Anon (the major support group for co-dependents) *says* that the co-dependent needs to focus upon her or his own disease, much of the *actual* focus is on how to live with an alcoholic.

I think the next phase in the development of this concept was recognizing that the enabler, or co-dependent, was also in a great deal of pain and needed help. Concurrently with this phase was the realization, statistically, that children of alcoholic families tended to become alcoholics and/or develop serious problems adjusting to life. We began to see that the disease process was perpetuating itself and that it functioned on a larger scale than we had previously thought.

Currently, we are beginning to recognize that co-dependence is a disease in its own right. It fits the disease concept in that it has an *onset* (a point at which the person's life is just not working, usually as a result of an addiction), a *definable course* (the person continues to deteriorate mentally, physically, psychologically, and spiritually), and, untreated, has a *predictable outcome* (death). We now know that co-dependence results in such physical complications as gastrointestinal problems, ulcers, high blood pressure, and even cancer. Indeed, the co-dependent will often die sooner than the chemically dependent person.

As a result of this progression within the CD field, co-dependence is now coming into its own as an area of concern and an area of specialization.

The Mental Health Field

The mental health field is yet another matter. Basically, the traditional specialties in the field of mental health have steadfastly refused to recognize the incidence, extent, and severity of addictions and co-dependence. Many traditional mental health professionals do not even know what co-dependence is. There are several reasons for this.

First, most mental health professionals learn little or nothing about addictions in their graduate training. As Charles Whitfield, a clinician and writer in the fields of chemical dependency and the family, states: "I estimate that today, conservatively, 80 percent of all helping professionals remain untrained in this crucial area."[1]

In fact, most mental health professionals have had a unit on alcoholism and/or addictions that makes us even more dangerous. We have just enough knowledge to think we know something, which successfully prevents us from confronting our ignorance.

Second, traditional mental health techniques and theories have been singularly unsuccessful in the treatment of addictions. Even so, many mental health professionals continue to receive exorbitant fees and schedule endless hours with persons who are making little or no progress. Through this process, the mental health professional exhibits one of the major characteristics of co-dependence itself—denial.

For example, I recently conferred with a professional who was seeing a couple for therapy. I had been working with the wife separately for some time, and I had seen the husband for a few sessions, although he had refused to come back when I confronted him about his alcohol and money addictions. He was, however, willing to see the other professional both alone and with his wife. During our conference, the professional complained that the couple was not making progress using his techniques—making lists of what they liked about each other, etc. When I suggested that he might not be treating the real problem, he replied that there was nothing wrong with his techniques. Unfortunately, he said, they had a chronic problem relationship and what could be expected?

When I asked him if he was familiar with the treatment of addictions, he told me that the subject had been included in his graduate program. I then began to discuss the work of Wegscheider-Cruse, Johnson, and Black with respect to the dynamics of the addictive family. He had never heard of their work, and he did not feel he needed to know about it, since he had been trained in family therapy and considered himself to be a family therapist. I asked if he was familiar with the Twelve Step program of Alcoholics Anonymous and Al-Anon. Again, his answer was yes, but he said that his clients were not "*the kind of people*" who needed to be involved in *that* (clearly revealing his ignorance).

So far, I was batting 1.000. When I asked if he was familiar with the term *co-dependence,* he said that he thought perhaps he had heard it, but he could not give me a *clear* definition of what it meant. I told him that I found it discouraging that when our joint client recommended that he read *Another Chance, I'll Quit Tomorrow,* and other pertinent material, he had done nothing. He became defensive, saying that I seemed to feel that I was superior to him. I told him that I thought he was acting unprofessionally in not becoming informed about an illness that obviously related to one of his clients, especially when this illness frequently results in death. I used diabetes as an analogy. If we had a joint client who had diabetes and if, in ignorance of the disease, he was recommending that the client continue to use sugar, I would be obliged to express my concern for the client's welfare. Unfortunately, this professional persisted in using techniques that denied the disease and were singularly unbeneficial to the client.

This pattern, I'm afraid, is typical of many in the mental health field. The technique is rarely wrong; the patient is simply "unworkable."

The third reason why the mental health approach to addictions is unsuccessful relates to a fact mentioned earlier—most mental health theories are developed by people who perceive themselves as free of any disease. Hence, the theories and techniques are developed abstractly, rationally, and logically, quite apart from the *experience* of the theorist. In fact, the validity of any theory is based on the non-involvement of the theorist, which provides the necessary "objectivity" and distance to treat the disease in that model. Unfortunately, this approach to developing theory is especially susceptible to certain aspects of the disease itself, such as denial, rationalization, "stinkin' thinkin'," the need to control, etc., none of which enhance treatment.

Despite all of these factors, traditional mental health professionals are now much more interested and involved in the field of addictions and co-dependence. There are several reasons for this.

The first is a humanitarian concern for healing in an area where a need is perceived. The mental health field sees that millions of people in this country are affected by addictions. An epidemic of this scope is bound to come to the attention of the medical and mental health professionals, as well it should.

Second, the treatment of addictions has become a big business. Addictive diseases have reached an epidemic proportion *and* not only derelicts but the wealthy and famous are admitting to problems with them. What was previously a field relegated to "quasi-professionals"—who themselves were recovering and who did not have graduate degrees—has suddenly become a multimillion-dollar concern. The development of theories and techniques had previously been left to persons who fit no major professional category or were not completely "within the fold," and the process of understanding the disease involved looking at it from within, not observing it from the outside. But because the treatment of addictions now involves money and prestige, traditional professionals believe that it should be within their domain, and so they are generating theories and techniques consistent with a mental health perspective.

Lastly is the issue of control. Who will control a treatment industry that is changing fast and has suddenly become very profitable? Will tradition prevail and will this field move under the control of the established professions? Will the group with the most viable and functional theory prevail? How does control relate to what has essentially been a nonprofit, volunteer movement (A.A.) with one of the best success rates of any approach to treating this disease?

Fortunately or not, the issues surrounding co-dependence are even less clear than those related to addictions themselves. Where does the co-dependent fall within the chemical dependency field? Is the treatment of co-dependence an adjunct to the treatment of addictions? Does the co-dependent really fit into traditional psychiatric and psychological categories and, if so, can she or he be treated using traditional approaches? Is it possible to put co-dependence within the traditional categories of diagnosis, even if it does not fit? Since co-dependence does not fall under the CD diagnosis, should it be treated by mental health professionals and, if so, how? Where does insurance coverage apply in this confusion? Many of these issues almost seem to overshadow effective treatment at times.

The Women's Movement

No discussion of the development of the concept of co-dependence would be complete without a reference to feminism and the women's movement.

Since many co-dependents are women, and since many women are thought to be co-dependent, women's issues are intimately related to co-dependence. In our attempts within the women's movement to understand and therefore free women, we have looked under many stones and found many addictions.

As we have tried to understand our lives and the influences upon them, we have had to look more closely at the factors that externally limit and control us. In order to do this, it has been necessary for us to describe our realities and the way we relate to them.[2] As we have delineated the forces that oppress us and contribute to our disease and unhealthiness, it is not surprising to find that those forces parallel the characteristics found in addiction and co-dependence. It seems to be no accident, then, that many of the characteristics of the nonliberated woman are also those that are emerging as characteristic of the (male or female) co-dependent: low self-esteem; passivity; not taking care of yourself physically, emotionally, spiritually, and/or psychologically;

compromising yourself; ignoring your personal morality; perfectionism; and so on.

Nor is it surprising that the women's movement, like the field of addictions and co-dependence, is a grass-roots movement, where knowledge is first developed by those who are affected and is *then* synthesized into theory, rather than being gleaned from analyzed material and objective data.

Hence, in mental health circles, the women's movement has borne the same stamp of illegitimacy as the chemical dependency field. As renegade enterprises, however, each field has much to offer the other. Much of what has been learned in one field is congruent with what is known in the other; each field helps clarify and inform the other.

Since I have been active in the women's movement, am a traditionally trained mental health professional and a trained family therapist, and am personally involved in the CD field as an actively recovering co-dependent, I hope to weave together what is most useful in each field into a comprehensive theory of co-dependence.

Before I do that, however, I want to comment on some of the best known conceptualizations of co-dependence and describe what I think is helpful and not helpful about them. Since so little has been written in this fast-growing field, I want to take the opportunity to recognize and summarize current thinking, as I understand it, and build my own theories upon present knowledge.

I agree that it is absolutely urgent that we recognize that persons who are around addictive behavior have a greater difficulty maintaining their own sobriety and are more likely to slide into their own disease, and it is important to recognize that it is their disease they are sliding into, not the disease of the alcoholic.

chapter two

The Range of Definitions of Co-Dependence

Little has been written about the various approaches to co-dependence and while the information about this disease is expanding at a rapid rate, much of it is available only in workshops or on audiotapes. Those of us working in the field and generating descriptions, data, and theory are often so involved in what we are doing that we have not taken the time to write down our ideas. Also—and I speak for myself here—since new insights and awarenesses are emerging constantly, the ideas do not yet seem complete enough to commit to paper.

In this chapter, I want to discuss some of the definitions of co-dependence that are most often articulated by the emerging theorists in the field. These persons are all contributing greatly to our understanding of this disease, and they have made valuable and important contributions to our knowledge. Each, however, has also missed significant pieces of the puzzle. I believe their omissions are partly a result of an incomplete understanding of the overall picture and of the underlying addictive process. I want to give credit to these pioneers in the field, however, and at the same time point out gaps that I think inhibit our understanding of this disease.

Wegscheider-Cruse

Sharon Wegscheider-Cruse is a social worker who has been a strong voice in developing the concept of co-dependence and providing treatment for co-dependents. In one of her workshops she has defined co-dependents as "all persons who (1) are in a love or marriage relationship with an alcoholic, (2) have one or more alcoholic parents or grandparents, or (3) grew up in an emotionally repressive family." According to Wegscheider-Cruse, this includes approximately 96 percent of the population.

In an essay in *Co-Dependency: An Emerging Issue*, she has further defined co-dependence as "a primary disease and a disease within every member of an alcoholic family."[1] She has also said that many alcoholics were co-dependents before they became alcoholics.

One of my difficulties with Wegscheider-Cruse's definitions is that they almost always make reference to the alcoholic. While she hints that the disease has a more pervasive aspect, it is not clear what she really means by this.

Smalley

Sondra Smalley, who conducts numerous workshops on co-dependence in the Minneapolis area and has written several pamphlets on the concept, has suggested in her workshops that "co-dependency is a pattern of learned behaviors, feelings, and beliefs that make life painful." She has further stated that the co-dependent is "human-relationship-dependent and focuses her/his life around an addictive agent." Again, I am sure that all of this is true, and yet something is missing. The above could be said for the alcoholic or the neurotic who is obsessive. Just what the difference is she does not make clear.

Smalley also appears to reject the disease concept of co-dependence. She clearly stated in one of her recent workshops that co-dependence is *not* an illness; she believes that it resembles a personality disorder but differs in that the co-dependent is still functional (as are most neurotics).

I think it would be a grave mistake to try to fit our perceptions of addictions and co-dependence—experientially gathered data—into typical DSM III categories, which depend on objective, linear, rational forms of data. The two are being conceptualized from very different systems and perspectives.

Subby

Robert Subby has defined co-dependence as "an emotional, psychological, and behavioral condition that develops as a result of an individual's prolonged exposure to, and practice of, a set of oppressive rules—rules which prevent the open expression of feeling as well as the direct discussion of personal and interpersonal problems."[2]

Subby is one of the few theorists who does not think co-dependence should be linked solely to alcoholism. He looks at it in a larger context. Coming out of a family therapy orientation, he has stated that co-dependence "is an emotional, psychological, and behavioral pattern of coping that is born of the rules of a family and not as a result of alcoholism."[3] This definition, I think, is much broader than the others I've examined, and yet it still fails to place co-dependence in its total cultural context, and it is not descriptive enough. Interestingly, Subby talks about the co-dependent who seeks a partner who "lives by a set of rules similar to his own."[4] How, may I ask, can one avoid finding such a person, if a vast majority of the population is co-dependent, as Wegscheider-Cruse and others have asserted? We really have not looked at the implications of this assertion.

In another article, Subby and John Friel have defined co-dependence as a "dysfunctional pattern of living and problem solving which is nurtured by a set of rules within the family system."[5] Among the rules are the following: (1) it's not okay to talk about problems; (2) feelings should not be expressed openly; (3) communication is best if indirect, with one person acting as messenger between two others (triangulation); (4) be strong, good, right, perfect; (5) make us proud (unrealistic expectations); (6) don't be selfish; (7) do as I say, not as I do; (8) it's not okay to play or be playful; and (9) don't rock the boat.

Here too Subby and Friel define the family as the primary system out of which personal behaviors evolve. I think the family is an *important* system, but I don't believe that it is the *primary* system. It is *one* of the primary systems, the others being the personal system (within the individual), the institutional system with which we must cope, and the society at large. While it may be true that co-dependence "originates in the family system,"[6] our understanding of this disease must look at more than the family system for us to understand it in its entirety and its context.

Whitfield

Charles Whitfield is a physician and writer who works extensively with addictions and teaches at the Johns Hopkins and the University of Maryland medical schools. Of all the approaches to co-dependence I've seen, Whitfield's takes in the immensity of the problem: "It [co-dependence] affects not only individuals, but families, communities, businesses and other institutions, and states and countries." Yet he still links the disease solely to alcohol. It is defined as "ill health, or maladaptive or problematic behavior that is associated with living, working with, or otherwise being close to a person with alcoholism." He equates "para-alcoholism," "co-alcoholism," "near-alcoholism," and "co-dependence."[7]

What we see in Whitfield is a broader perspective within a constricted context. I agree that it is absolutely urgent that we recognize that persons who are around addictive behavior have a greater difficulty maintaining *their* own sobriety and are more likely to slide into *their* own disease, *and* it is important to recognize that it is their disease they are sliding into, *not* the disease of the alcoholic. Even though Whitfield does not state it, he seems to come dangerously close to saying that co-alcoholism or co-dependence is something that is "caught" from the alcoholic or is part of the contagion of alcoholism. I believe that it is more accurate to say that the disease of co-dependence was present before alcoholism emerged, and when it is untreated and triggered, it emerges.

Larsen

Earnie Larsen, who also lives in the Twin Cities and is a counselor, has made several tapes on co-dependence and has published a book on *Stage II Recovery*. In a 1983 tape on the *Basics of Co-Dependency*, he defined the co-dependent as "anyone who has been *affected* by the person who has been *afflicted* by the disease of chemical dependency." He extends his definition to include "anyone who lives in close association over a prolonged time with anyone who has a neurotic personality."[8] Larsen's definition appears to focus on the fact that the co-dependent has been affected. Interestingly enough, he has further suggested that there are between ten and fifteen million alcoholics in this society and that each one directly and adversely *affects* between twenty and thirty persons. Using his figures, and not accounting for any overlap, we see that the number of co-dependents in the United States exceeds the total population. Interesting and impressive!

I think, though, that Larsen's emphasis on the notion of being *affected* is misleading here. This emphasis makes co-dependence also sound like some form of contagion— like something that is transmitted and "caught." It also makes the alcoholic somehow responsible, either overtly or covertly, for another's co-dependence. I believe that we are indeed affected and also, paradoxically, that we already have a latent disease that is triggered when we are affected.

•   •

Some very interesting questions arise from an examination of these definitions. Is what we are identifying as co-dependence always related to alcohol? Larsen and Wegscheider-Cruse seem to think not. Larsen extends his definition to include anyone who is *affected* by a neurotic, and Wegscheider-Cruse extends hers to include anyone who grew up in an emotionally repressive family. Both develop the concept to the point that it includes the majority of the population of the United States. Subby extends his definition to describe family rules that appear to be the statistical "norm" for this society, and Whitfield includes "institutions, states and countries" in his list of affected parties. What do we do with all of this?

Clearly, each person cited here is talking about something specific and something general. I believe that both qualities are important. Paradoxically, what they are talking about is at the same time the specific *and* the general. I think that what many of the definitions described here touch on is a conceptualization that there is a disease process that underlies both alcoholism and co-dependence. This basic disease process is what I would call the *addictive process*. Let us explore this notion further.

*An addiction is anything we feel we have
to lie about.*

chapter three

Co-Dependence: A Disease
Within the Addictive Process

It is easy to see from my previous discussion of the histor-
ical development and some current definitions of co-dependence that theorists are moving towards broader definitions
of this disease *and* trying to treat the specific problems
inherent in living with and/or relating to a person who is
chemically dependent.

I would like to suggest that what we are calling co-
dependence is, indeed, a *disease* that has many forms and
expressions and that grows out of a disease process that is
inherent in the system in which we live. I call this disease
process the *addictive process*.

The addictive process is an unhealthy and abnormal
disease process, whose assumptions, beliefs, behaviors, and
lack of spirituality lead to a process of nonliving that is progressively death-oriented. This basic disease, from which
spring the subdiseases of co-dependence and alcoholism—
among others—is tacitly and openly supported by the society
in which we live.

I also believe that trying to generate definitions from a
rational, logical premise is actually a manifestation of the
disease process. I want to avoid that sort of analysis. I will

attempt to describe, discuss, and list the characteristics of co-dependence while also examining this sub-disease within the larger context of the addictive process in our culture.

It is my belief that many diseases and psychological and behavioral difficulties are manifestations of the addictive process. All of these diseases and difficulties have some characteristics in common; other characteristics are specific to the subdisease or are manifested in a way that is peculiar to a particular subdisease.

In order to clarify the basic disease (the addictive process) and its subdiseases, I offer the diagram on page 27. The purpose of this diagram is not to show the characteristics of the basic disease, but to show how different subdiseases are manifestations of the same basic disease, as perceived from different perspectives and as labeled by different professions. The perspectives that I will focus on are the fields of chemical dependency and mental health, the women's movement, and family therapy.

It is absolutely crucial that we see that the syndromes described earlier (and shown in the diagram) stem from a common disease process and that this disease process is systemic to our society! To ignore this fact is to stay isolated in our areas of specialty and miss the big picture.

The CD Field

Within the chemical dependency field, an addiction is broadly considered to be the compulsive need for any substance or process outside the person that becomes more important than sobriety—the state of functioning in a way that is clear, healthy, and normal for the human organism. (Sobriety can also be defined as a person's living process and/or spirituality.)

The Addictive Process—A Generic, Systemic Disease

Chemical Dependency	Mental Health	Women's Movement	Family Therapy
• Alcoholism	• Character Disorders	• Nonliberated Man	• Dysfunctional Family
• Drug Addiction	• Certain Psychoses (manic depression)	• Nonliberated Woman	• Chemically Dependent Family
• Eating Disorders	• Narcissistic Personality		
• Sexual Addictions	• Obsessive-Compulsive Personality		
• Gambling Addictions	• Dependent Personality		
• Co-Dependence —Para-alcoholism —Co-alcoholism —Addictive Relationships	• Depression		
	• Antisocial-Psychopathic Personality		
	• Phobias		
	• Inadequate Personality		
	• Conversion Disorders		

An addiction to food and/or chemicals is often called an ingestive addiction. A process addiction is an addiction (by individuals, groups, or even societies) to a way (or the process) of acquiring the addictive substance. The function of an addiction is to keep us out of touch with ourselves (our feelings, morality, awareness—our living process). An addiction, in short, is any substance or process we feel we have to lie about.

In the chemical dependency field, it is common knowledge that giving up the chemical of choice is always just the tip of the iceberg. Almost always, recovering persons, after giving up the chemical that is killing them most obviously and most effectively, quickly begin to use other chemicals (usually ones that are not such fast killers, such as nicotine, caffeine, or sugar) just as addictively. This behavior supports the idea that we are not just treating a particular chemical addiction, but are actually working with an addictive process from which many addictions can stem.

The same may be said for the co-dependent and/or enabler. The untreated, unrecovered, nonsober enabler may well get out of the destructive relationship with the alcoholic only to fall into the same kind of relationship with children, friends, and/or a new spouse.

Moreover, we all know people who are recovering from their alcoholism and who are described as nonrecovering co-dependents. One of my friends, who is a recovering alcoholic, doing well with her recovery and having no trouble avoiding alcohol, said to me once, "Dealing with the alcoholism is the *easy* part, but dealing with the insidiousness of my co-dependence is really difficult." I think she is talking about her *addictive process*. She told me that she could understand why people said that they were "grateful" alcoholics. In recovery, the chemical served many useful functions: (1) it forced her into treatment; (2) it gave her something concrete that she knew she had to give up or die; (3) it gave her a group of people (through A.A.) with whom she could identify and from whom she could get immense support; and (4) it provided her with a set of tools (the Twelve Steps of A.A.), which promised, if she used them, a process of recovery.

Co-dependence was not like that. When my friend slipped into her co-dependent (addictive process) behavior, she felt just as sick and crazy as she did when she was drinking, and yet she did not experience the clarity of the problem or the support she had in her recovery from alcoholism. In fact, it almost seemed that those around her expected and supported her addictive process and were upset when she did not enable! Interesting! She was recovering from her addiction to the chemical, but she was not recovering (or at least she was not recovering as well and not as clearly) from the disease that was behind the use of the addictive substance.

All of us who work in this field and who work with co-dependents are familiar with the concept of the "dry drunk." A "dry drunk" is a person who exhibits the behaviors, attitudes, and thinking associated with the active disease of alcoholism—without using the chemical. This syndrome is also described as the loss of sobriety, the loss of abstinence, and "getting into the disease" in chemical dependency circles. An individual on a dry drunk is not using the ingestive agent and yet is acting as if she or he were. And life with the addict may be worse for the addict's family *after* she or he gives up the chemical. It is at this point, I believe, that the basic disease of the addictive process surfaces in all its insidiousness. The chemical that masked it is no longer present, and the underlying disease emerges unchecked. To see the dry drunk as a bursting forth out of the basic disease offers a good explanation of a phenonmenon that we have frequently observed.

The notion that there is an addictive process lurking *behind* alcoholism would also explain why the A.A. Twelve Step program is so essential and successful in treating the disease. We all know that not drinking, for example, does not constitute recovery. We also know that just going to meetings does not work. We know too that "conning" the program and not really "working" it does not work and is, in fact, practicing the disease. In order to become sober and maintain sobriety, a person has to make major changes in her or his attitudes, beliefs, behavior, thinking, and practice. This is not only true for the alcoholic or addict; it is also necessary for the co-dependent, the relationship addict, the food addict, and all other addicts. What the A.A. Twelve Step program does, I believe, is facilitate what I call a *systems change*. The Twelve Step program is a set of tools to bring about a change from an *addictive system* to a *living process system,* which is a system we all know but have been trained out of. (I will discuss the living process system in more detail in Chapter 5.)

Because the Twelve Step program is so vital to recovery, I want to list the steps here.[1] My comments about each step follow the list.

The Twelve Steps

1. We admitted we were powerless over alcohol—that our lives had become unmanageable.
2. Came to believe that a Power Greater than Ourselves could restore us to sanity.
3. Made a decision to turn our will and our lives over to the care of *God as we understood Him.*
4. Made a searching and fearless moral inventory of ourselves.

5. Admitted to God, to ourselves and to another human being the exact nature of our wrongs.

6. Were entirely ready to have God remove all these defects of character.

7. Humbly asked Him to remove our shortcomings.

8. Made a list of all persons we had harmed, and became willing to make amends to them all.

9. Made direct amends to such people wherever possible, except when to do so would injure them or others.

10. Continued to take personal inventory and when we were wrong promptly admitted it.

11. Sought through prayer and meditation to improve our conscious contact with God as we understood Him, praying only for knowledge of His will for us and the power to carry that out.

12. Having had a spiritual awakening as a result of these steps, we tried to carry this message to others, and to practice these principles in all our affairs.

Comments

1. "Alcohol," or our co-dependence, our controlling behavior, our fears, etc.—anything that makes our lives unmanageable.

2. Not only a statement of faith but also an admission that how we are operating lacks sanity.

3. Some people say our Higher Power or Power Greater than Ourselves; some say our living process; some say our spirituality. Whatever works. The original wording is sexist and limited.

4. This step has to be "worked" and takes time, thoroughness, and effort, and it means working our "positives" as well as our "negatives."

5. This means going over Step Four with a sponsor or spiritual advisor.

6. This is not as easy as it sounds—most of our "character defects" are "old friends," or have been survival mechanisms, like stubbornness, dishonesty, etc.

7. As stated above, this is not easy; these shortcomings usually have been our survival techniques. They're not techniques for *living*, however!

8. *All*—this needs to be thorough and ongoing.

9. It is important not to be self-centered with this step and "inflict" others with our amends.

10. This is an ongoing *process*.

11. "Prayer and meditation," or however you do this. "Contact with God," or contact with our spirituality. "Knowledge of his will for us"—to live out of our spiritual lives and selves or, as I would say it, our "living process."

12. Not *inflict* it on others, but offer it in a respectful way; this is difficult for people who tend to be controlling.

It is important to say here that the Twelve Steps are not linear; they are a process. You work through them and simultaneously rework them, and the process helps move us out of an addictive system into a living process system. I firmly believe that since most people in this society are trained into an addictive system and the addictive process, most people could benefit from working a Twelve Step program, or something similar to it.

In some treatment circles, we have been saying that the disease of alcoholism and the disease of co-dependence (or co-alcoholism or para-alcoholism) is, in essence, the same disease. The disease manifests itself in different ways, and yet it displays some of the same elements (to be discussed in detail in Chapter 4). I believe that this idea supports the concept that I am proposing, that both alcoholism and co-dependence do indeed come from the same stem and are manifestations of the same thing. Both diseases are amenable to the Twelve Step program. Indeed, we are seeing a tremendous proliferation of Twelve Step programs for persons with eating disorders, parenting problems, sex problems, relationship problems, and so on. The fact that so many people are voluntarily involving themselves in these programs and getting better because of them seems to me to support the concept of a basic disease underlying all of the addictions and addiction-related diseases.

Another development in the CD field that supports the idea of a basic disease is the recently articulated notion that *everyone* who works with, lives with, or is around an alcoholic (or a person actively in an addictive process) is by *definition* a co-dependent and a practicing co-dependent. This includes therapists, counselors, ministers, colleagues, *and* the family. As I stated earlier, these people are not *just* being affected; they are also slipping into *their* disease and losing their own sobriety. We used to say (and some still do) that at least seven to ten people were negatively affected by the alcoholic (and Earnie Larsen suggests twice that number). This observation has some truth to it. Unfortunately, it still puts the focus on the alcoholic and makes the alcoholic the reference point. I have discovered that when I am working a good program, staying sober, and in tune with my own process, the alcoholic can stand on her or his head, turn green, and do all sorts of antics and I will be unaffected. Ultimately I have to leave my sobriety to "get into *my* disease"; it is not the alcoholic who gets me into my disease. This, somehow, says to me that the underlying disease is there, systemic, and internally available to most people in the society. We also frequently believe the alcoholic was alcoholic before she or he ever found the chemical, which also supports the idea of an underlying disease process.

I believe that all of the examples cited above support my contention that we are, indeed, dealing with a broad systemic disease from which specific addictions and dependencies arise.

The Mental Health Field

I am appalled by the basic ignorance about addictions and co-addictions in the mental health field. Charles Whitfield believes that all untreated and/or untrained people in the general population are affected by the addictive system (he doesn't call it by this name), whether or not they are closely related to or associated with an alcoholic. This observation leads him to believe that we must look carefully at what he calls the "untrained" and/or "untreated professional"— professionals who are not themselves aware of the diseases of the addictive process or co-dependence and therefore are not dealing with it in themselves.[2] He estimates, as I note in Chapter 1, that this includes 80 percent of all helping professionals. I agree with him and take this idea a step further by pointing out that our awareness that those who are operating in the addictive process and not actively recovering from it are, at many levels, perpetuating this disease. To me, this is a staggering idea.

There is another conclusion to be drawn, namely, that a large number of professionals are themselves active addicts and/or co-dependents. Since mental health theories are generally proposed by people who believe themselves to be objective and free of any disease, these theorists have often denied the very basis of the disease (unconsciously, I presume). In spite of this, they have made observations and developed concepts that help define *aspects* of the co-dependence, yet they fail to see the disease in the context of addictions.

Having originally been trained in the traditional mental health field, I have had to learn about the chemical dependency field as I became involved and progressively more interested in it. As I became more aware of the CD field, I noticed that many mental health concepts are incorporated in the CD field, and the diseases are often better explained and better treated there.

For example, there is a growing body of literature in the mental health field about narcissism. In fact, there has been a proliferation of theories about it. I find that the concept of self-centeredness often used in CD circles is essentially the same concept, and I also observe that it is handled in a much more practical and effective way there. In the CD field, narcissism (or self-centeredness) is linked directly with the disease of alcoholism and/or co-dependence, and it is treated, as a character defect, with the Twelve Step program. Intellectualizing about it is not and has never been effective. The important point is, however, that both theoretical approaches are observing and noting the same phenomenon and are just labeling it differently.

Psychological and psychiatric literature is replete with concepts that parallel those in the CD field—the dependent personality, the obsessive-compulsive personality, phobias, depression, inadequate personalities, character disorders, and even psychosis, to name a few. This suggests to me that even though these two fields are describing the same phenomena, it is likely that they have named and are treated these syndromes quite differently.

Let me give a couple of examples from my own clinical experience. When I was first getting acquainted with the field of chemical dependency, I was so fascinated with some of the ideas (as I still am!) that I was eager to discuss them whenever I could. Once, when I was on a plane, I started discussing the topic with a man sitting next to me, who I soon learned was the director of a mental health clinic. As I was excitedly sharing my new discoveries, he made a statement that astonished me. He said that whenever *anyone* came to the clinic with a presenting symptom of depression, the staff routinely screened that person and her or his family for chemical dependency. I thought this was quite inventive and asked him what he usually found. He said that in about 90 percent of the cases there was, in fact, some readily diagnosable chemical dependency problem! I was impressed. The clinic then treated the chemical dependency or the co-dependence as primary. How different from using antidepressant drugs or long-term psychotherapy or even shock therapy!

To take another example, several years ago I began seeing a young man in therapy. He had been a bright, effective scholar and leader in high school and had seemingly fallen apart when he went to college. By the time I started seeing him, some years after that, he had been diagnosed as manic-depressive, had had at least two "psychotic breaks," and was taking lithium. I had been trained in the years before lithium and had been taught that manic-depressive psychosis was very rare. Perhaps because of this and perhaps because as I went over his records and met with his psychiatrist, I did not think he seemed like a typical manic-depressive, so I worked with his M.D. and we eventually terminated his medication. There were no clinical changes as a result of this termination, and I continued to see him in individual therapy. He gradually improved and, since he had no relapses, he terminated his therapy.

I knew little or nothing about chemical dependency at the time (I *thought* I did). Several years later, after I had become knowledgeable in the field, this man came to see me again because of some problems he was having. I now saw his problems as typical of addictive behavior, and I zeroed in on possible addictions. His chemical of choice was marijuana, although he thought that he probably had a drinking problem, too. After several explorations with A.A. and the Twelve Step program, he decided that he felt more comfortable with Narcotics Anonymous and focused on those meetings. His therapy became an adjunct to his Twelve Step program, as I think it should be in early recovery. After he had dealt with his addiction to marijuana, we then worked through his addictions to alcohol, nicotine, caffeine, sugar (he was badly hypoglycemic), money, and relationships. The Twelve Step program provided the focus, and his therapy provided the avenue both to work with a complex constellation of addictions and, simultaneously, to treat the addictive process. The combination proved powerful for him and he is doing very well. I really believe that had I continued to treat him with traditional mental health approaches, he probably would have, at best, maintained, and he may have been rediagnosed as having an "inadequate personality," a less serious condition. But I do not think he would have been the fully functioning member of society that he is now.

At least two threads can be teased out of these two examples. First, knowledge of addictions and the addictive process is very important for mental health practitioners. Second, some of the symptoms, characteristics, and dynamics that I have isolated in my discussion of mental health may actually be manifestations of the basic addictive process.

The Women's Movement

As I have said before, no discussion of the disciplines that are quite separately discovering and developing these similar concepts is complete unless we look at the ideas that have come out of the concern for women's and men's liberation. Disparate groups have observed the same phenomena and are making interpretations based upon their particular biases.

For example, Kathy Cappell-Sowder describes the developing co-dependent in this way: "As the alcoholic becomes increasingly preoccupied with getting, using, and keeping the alcohol, the 'developing co-dependent' becomes more focused on that person, his behavior, and his chemical use, and begins to change her own behavior in response to the alcoholic's lifestyle. Behavior changes may include efforts to check on or control the drinking or drinking-related friends or activities ('protecting her supply'), peacekeeping within the family system, isolation from activities outside the family, basically adding up to focusing on the drinker himself (the definition of addiction), and a lifestyle centered around him."[3]

As I read this description of the budding codependent, I was painfully aware that, if the references to alcohol or drinking were omitted, it was easily interchangeable with a feminist's definition of a nonliberated woman or a nonliberated man.

The nonliberated woman or man is dependent, self-centered, externally referented, out of touch with her or his feelings, etc., just as the addict and the co-dependent are. Once again, the same syndrome is being described from a different perspective. The characteristics of the nonliberated woman are identical to the characteristics of the co-dependent. The nonliberated woman (or the nonliberated man) is to the macho man (or the nonliberated woman) what the co-dependent woman is to the alcoholic man. No matter how the roles are switched around, the picture is the same.

In *Women's Reality,* I described what I then called the Ideal American Marriage as having exactly the same elements as what I would now call an addictive relationship. The Ideal American Marriage is based upon mutual dependency: neither partner can function without the other. The lives of the married couple are totally intertwined, and much is sacrificed for the illusion of security (control and sameness). The assumption made is that if each partner is made totally dependent upon the other, neither will leave and both will have security. After a while in this kind of arrangement, neither *can* leave because neither can function without the other. This is addiction!

When we look closely at the sort of woman that the women's movement wants to liberate, we see the perfect co-dependent. She gets her identity completely from outside herself; she has no self-esteem or self-worth; she is isolated from her feelings; and she spends much of her time trying to figure out what others want so she can give it to them. She is lonely because she is estranged from herself. She is controlling because she has no self and is so dependent upon others. Her entire life is devoted to her husband and her children, and yet she is experienced by others as self-centered and controlling. The nonliberated woman and the co-dependent are the same person. The only difference is that the women's movement has approached co-dependence as a women's issue. It *is* that and more. Sexism, racism, ageism, and homophobia are outgrowths of an addictive society.

As we learn more about chemical dependency, we begin to see that many of the cultural issues that concern the women's movement are also visible when we look at chemical dependency and co-dependence within their cultural context. The women's movement is concerned about violence, especially towards women and children; increasingly, we are seeing that domestic violence is almost always related to addictive relationships or the use of chemicals.

The women's movement asserts the right of women to own and protect their own bodies; possessiveness (of another) is a characteristic of an addictive system. The women's movement is concerned about the invisibility of women; the co-dependent is completely overshadowed by her spouse's alcoholism. (Al-Anon focuses on rebuilding a woman's self-identity and having her take responsibility for her own life.) The nonliberated woman gets her power from overt and covert control of her environment; so does the co-dependent. We are looking at the same syndrome approached from different perspectives.

Although I have focused on the nonliberated woman, I believe there are parallels in the concerns of the men's movement for what is happening to men in the culture. I also believe that it is easy to demonstrate that many of the characteristics of the nonliberated man also describe the chemically dependent or co-dependent person. For example, the macho man is not in touch with his feelings (and he often uses chemicals to numb them), and he spends much of his time doing what is called "impression management"— trying to make others see him as he wants to be seen and believing that he can control their impressions. Because his point of reference is external, he too has lost his identity. The nonliberated man overworks, overdrinks, and overeats, pushing himself to an early death. He becomes a zombie, who moves through life and does not live it. His dishonesty with himself extends to his relationships, his business dealings, and his entire life. He exhibits the same characteristics as the chemically dependent person does and these characteristics are precisely the focus of the men's movement. They are dealing, in fact, with the same syndrome. The labels are different; the focus is different; the perspective is different; *and* it is the same systemic disease.

Both men and women are being destroyed by their involvement in this syndrome. Both are affected by the generic disease we have called the addictive process, the disease out of which co-dependence and these more specific subsyndromes emerge.

Family Therapy

Family therapy is the last discipline I want to focus on in my attempt to demonstrate that each of these approaches has been looking at the same syndrome. Family therapists have been instrumental in acknowledging the disease of co-dependence, and their concern for the plight of those related to the chemically dependent person has been crucial.

Yet—and this may be hard for some of us to believe— family therapy *did* have life before its involvement in chemical dependency, and many family therapists have no formal knowledge of either chemical dependency or co-dependence, and so they do not treat them. However, what family therapists describe as the dysfunctional family system is essentially the same as what family program counselors call the chemically dependent family system. The roles described in each system are essentially the same. For example:

- The *identified patient* in the dysfunctional family is the person who has obvious problems (but is not the only person in the family with problems) and is responsible for bringing the family into treatment. This role is analogous in the chemically dependent family to the *addict,* who is obviously ill, but is certainly not the only person needing help in a chemically dependent family system.

- The *hero* plays essentially the same role in both dysfunctional and the chemically dependent families. The hero, who is often the spouse and/or one of the children (usually the firstborn), holds the family together and keeps it functioning, even at a low level.

- In CD circles, we often hear about the *lost child*, the child who causes no trouble and basically disappears. Lost children frequently establish little or no self-identity, and they often display, more blatantly than the other children, the characteristics of the child of an alcoholic. In a dysfunctional family, a similar role is played by the *withdrawn* or *silent child*.

- Both family therapists and CD counselors recognize a role known as the *scapegoat*, which is sometimes played by the identified patient in a dysfunctional family. The scapegoat does the acting-out in both family systems and is always getting into trouble, frequently in school and with the law.

- In both family systems, there is usually a *comic* (in the dysfunctional family) or a *mascot* (in a chemically dependent family), each of whom plays the role of reducing stress through humor. This person relieves tension and is essential to keeping the family system limping along.

The point I want to make here is that the same conceptualizations are used by family therapy and chemical dependency counselors, and both professions, I believe, are dealing with the same phenomena. Both the dysfunctional family system and the chemically dependent family system are closed and operate by a set of rules that inhibit growth and are destructive to those in the system. However, what is crucially missing in family therapy is the awareness that the family and the therapist are first and foremost dealing with *addictions*. Without an understanding of the addictive process, traditional family therapy is not very effective in treating chemical dependency and co-dependence. Family therapists *can* help families clear up communication patterns, deal with coalitions, learn about roles, focus on positive feelings, and so on, but unless they treat the addiction, they are only applying a band-aid.

This is another case in which a discipline has looked at a specific problem from its own perspective and is describing what is essentially an outgrowth of an underlying disease syndrome.

•   •

In summary, I think the preceding discussion clearly supports my observation that we are dealing with an underlying, generic disease syndrome that has various manifestations and is inherent in the basic culture as we now know it and as it now functions. There are few, if any of us, not affected by this disease.

Probably apropos of this is the example of the way science approaches the development of theory. Frequently, the existence of a phenomenon is assumed because of its effect, not because it can be directly observed. For example, the existence of electrons, protons and neutrons, and black holes was postulated long before we could observe them, because we saw their effects and knew that a theory had to be developed to explain the observed effect. I believe that we are at the same point in generating our theories about the addictive process. Isolated groups have been observing the effects of this phenomenon. Because of their isolation from one another (and probably also because of their involvement in the practice of this disease), they have not seen that all these observations point to an underlying disease. I believe that we now have enough information to infer this basic, generic disease—the *addictive process*.

Co-dependence has no respect for age, color, social standing, or sex.

chapter four

The Characteristics of Co-Dependence

In this chapter I want to delineate some of the major characteristics of the addictive process and then describe these characteristics as they evidence themselves in the subdisease of co-dependence.

Each subsyndrome of the addictive process (like alcoholism, co-dependence, eating disorders) plays out the characteristics in a way that is specific to and peculiar to that subsyndrome. Not every characteristic is prominent in each subsyndrome, and each subsyndrome may also include some characteristics that are basically peculiar to it and are not delineated here. However, all of what will be described, I believe, points to a basic disease (the addictive process) and a subsyndrome of that process (in this case, co-dependence). As I have said earlier, in order to work with the subsyndrome effectively, we must treat both the general and the specific.

Characteristics of the Addictive Process

The following characteristics exist in the systemic disease of the addictive process. Not all of them exist in all the subsyndromes diagrammed in Chapter 3 (p. 27), and yet each syndrome listed on that diagram exhibits a cluster of these characteristics, which is enough to link it to the basic disease syndrome. Also, each subsyndrome has its unique form of the basic characteristics, which merits its being treated, paradoxically, as part of the general syndrome and as a unique disease. It would be a mistake to work with the syndrome as just an addictive process or as just a unique disease. It must be treated as both. Many of the characteristics named below will be explored further under the characteristics of co-dependence.

- Dishonesty (denial, projection, delusion)
- Not Dealing with Feelings in a Healthy Way (frozen feelings; being out of touch with feelings; distorted feelings; holding onto feelings, like resentment)
- Control
- Confusion
- Thinking Disorders (ego-oriented; confused thinking; obsessive thinking; overreliance on linear, logical, analytic thinking; dualistic—either/or—thinking)
- Perfectionism
- External Referenting—being "other-directed" (low self-worth, "impression management," shame-based existence)
- Dependency Issues
- Fear
- Rigidity
- Judgmentalism
- Depression
- Inferiority/Grandiosity
- Self-Centeredness

- Loss of Personal Morality (compromised value system, loss of a spiritual base)

- Stasis

- Negativism

   This is not an exhaustive list of the characteristics of the addictive process,[1] but it is extensive, as you can see. In earlier chapters, I have noted that in certain fields (like mental health, the women's and men's movement, and family therapy) the discussion of various problems has failed to see addiction as the center around which all these other syndromes pivot. As long as we practice our denial in this area, we will never see the whole picture. As Masanobu Fukuoka says in *The One Straw Revolution*, "An object seen in isolation from the whole is not the real thing."[2]

   There are many, many co-dependents in this society. The disease has no respect for age, color, social standing, or sex; it touches everyone in the society in one way or another. In one of her publications, Sharon Wegscheider-Cruse lists what she considers to be the high-risk groups for co-dependence: spouses of addicts; recovering addicts; adult children of alcoholics; young children with workaholic parents, grandparents, or siblings; and professionals who work with addictive persons. She also includes families with a secret or trauma, families that do not foster autonomy, and families that reward learned helplessness.[3] On one of his tapes, Earnie Larsen includes persons living with a neurotic.

   In this chapter, I want to explore how some of these characteristics emerge, cluster, and play themselves out in the disease of co-dependence. Since I will discuss frozen feelings, perfectionism, dishonesty, and thinking disorders in Chapter 5, I'll not develop them in detail here. Remember that we are dealing with a systemic disease, and we are also dealing with a specific form that requires and demands specific treatment.

Characteristics of Co-Dependence

• External Referenting

In this section I want to look at how co-dependents see themselves in relation to the world and how that way of seeing themselves manifests itself in co-dependence. External referenting is the most central characteristic of the addictive process that is exhibited in the disease of co-dependence. Some popular mimeographed lists of the characteristics of co-dependence, in fact, contain nothing but examples of this characteristic. It *is* probably the most important characteristic of the disease, and I think others are important also. We will explore it first because of its importance.

Relationship Addiction

Co-dependents are relationship addicts who frequently use a relationship in the same way drunks use alcohol: to get a "fix." Since co-dependents feel they have no intrinsic meaning of their own, almost all of their meaning comes from outside; they are almost completely externally referented. Persons who are so completely externally referented will do almost anything to be in a relationship, regardless of how awful the relationship is. Co-dependents have no concept of a self that others could relate to; whatever small vestige of the self does exist is easily given away in order to maintain a relationship because they feel like literally nothing without the relationship. I have seen many recovering co-dependents avoid intimate relationships in early recovery because they simply do not know how to form them without giving away big pieces of themselves in the process. Frequently, their partners are not asking them to give themselves away; co-dependents do it without being asked.

A friend was raised in an alcoholic family. She had grown up being trained into co-dependence (this is true for most children of alcoholics), and she had never known a relationship that did not require her to give up herself in order to survive. It was not until she was almost five years into her active recovery that she began to feel that she had developed enough of a self even to have friends. She was still not ready for an intimate love relationship! She was just starting to learn what it meant to have a self with which she could relate to others; she was also learning that not all relationships would require what her family had required—an abandonment of self.

Cling-Clung Relationships

In a cling-clung relationship, neither party can survive without the other, a condition that provides the relationship with security. This kind of security, however, which will be bought at any cost, is static and nongrowing. A great deal of energy is put into keeping a cling-clung relationship together, frequently at great personal cost to the co-dependent.

Lack of Boundaries

Co-dependents literally do not know where they end and others begin. One of my colleagues described this aspect of co-dependence as getting confused when others are confused. She said that she can be as clear as a bell one moment and then know she is slipping into her disease of co-dependence when she is around others who are confused and begins taking on their confusion as her own. This also applies to depression, anger, happiness—anything that one "takes on" from others without at the same time being clear that it is also coming from within. Some authors believe this is the crux of co-dependence. I think it is one major aspect of the disease.

Since they have no boundaries, co-dependents take on another's sadness, happiness, fear, or whatever people around them are feeling and/or thinking. I think we will see in Chapter 5 how three of our major institutions—the family, the school, and the church—actively train us not to form boundaries. They teach us to think what we are told to think, feel what we are told to feel, see what we are told to see, and know what we are told to know. This is cultural co-dependence training. We learn that the reference point for thinking, feeling, seeing, and knowing is external to the self, and this training produces people without boundaries. In order to have and experience boundaries, a person must start with an internal referent (knowing what one feels and thinks from the inside) and then relate with the world from that perspective.

Here is an example of how a lack of boundaries shows itself in co-dependence. The husband of one of my clients felt that two of their friends didn't like him, since they were not "doing things as couples anymore." He dispatched his wife (my client) to find out if his interpretation was correct, and amazingly she was willing to perform the task! This is indeed double co-dependence. Although my client did not think that the other couple disliked her spouse, she was willing to address the issue with them because her spouse was uncomfortable bringing the subject up. This is a good example of fused boundaries in a co-dependent relationship. Neither person knew where she or he ended and the other began; if one had a problem, they both had a problem. If one needed a clarification, they both needed a clarification. Her spouse was not taking responsibility for himself and his feelings, and she was practicing her co-dependence by her willingness to become involved *for* her spouse. Each had lost an awareness of the other's boundaries. They were fused.

I believe that examining this condition helps us understand why co-dependents have such great difficulty with intimacy. In order to be intimate, you need a self. Otherwise, getting close to another person always offers the possibility of being swallowed up by that person. Not knowing where you end and the other begins prevents a healthy coming-together, because coming-together always means fusion and being swallowed up.

I was once in a relationship in which my partner constantly accused me of wanting to swallow him up. I resisted this interpretation because it never felt accurate to me. One day he came home quite excited after a session with his therapist. "You know how I am always accusing you of wanting to swallow *me* up?" he asked. I said I did. He went on to report that he and his therapist had decided that this was not true at all. (I decided I really liked his therapist!) They had, however, decided that he really would like to swallow me up and had been projecting this desire onto me. (He was an adult child of an alcoholic. I was not.) From this example, we get a good picture of a boundary problem combined with the defense mechanism of projection. Staying clear of that combination is almost impossible for a co-dependent.

I think a lack of boundaries is easily seen in the alcoholic family. In the alcoholic family, everyone takes on the drinker's problem. In fact, the entire life of the family begins to revolve around the drinker. The co-dependents in the family give the alcoholic the power to define them and determine their moods and reactions. As the disease progresses, the boundaries become more and more blurred.

People who have no boundaries tend to personalize everything that happens around them and see it as directly related to them. Hence anything that happens must, by definition, be related to them.

Impression Management

Another form of external referenting is impression management, which is also a form of control but will be treated here because external referenting is so central to co-dependence. Since co-dependents have established no effective internal referents, it is absolutely necessary that others see them the way they want to be seen. Co-dependents are always trying to be "good" persons, and they actually believe that they can control others' perceptions.

The lives of co-dependents are structured by the question, "What will others think?" Co-dependents are insecure and have such low self-esteem that they must depend on others to prove their worth. Their main goal in life is to try to figure out what others want and then deliver that to them, for co-dependents are people-pleasers. They have developed amazing abilities to learn about the likes and dislikes of other people, and they truly believe that if they can just become what others want, they will be safe and accepted.

I once worked with a woman who was an expert at this behavior. She was very quiet and would sit and observe others' interactions for long periods of time. Once she had figured out what (she thought) their expectations were and how she was supposed to interact, she would participate. I became acutely aware of this pattern when I discovered that she never seemed to have a thought of her own; she would only paraphrase what I said. When I pointed that out, she was terrified. Her terror related to a budding awareness that she did not really believe or experience that she existed. Almost all of her information came from outside, and she knew no way to interact out of her own person. At that point, I believe that she did not know whether she, in fact, had "her own person."

Co-dependents are totally dependent on others for their very right to exist. If they are not validated and approved from the outside, they think they do not even have a right to be on this planet. Their code words are "I'm sorry," which really mean that they are sorry they exist at all.

I was recently at a restaurant with one of my friends, who struggles with her co-dependence at times. After our meal, the waiter came by and asked if we wanted anything more. I ordered a ginger ale, and she asked if he could bring her an iced tea. When he brought her tea, he realized he had forgotten to bring my ginger ale and had to go back for it. My friend's first response was, "I'm sorry." I could not imagine what she was sorry about and asked her. She explained that I had ordered first and she had tagged her order onto mine, so she was sorry that her drink had come first, a reaction that demonstrates how far she was into her disease of co-dependence. She could not control the waiter, nor could she control my potential anger (I had none)! I was not going to sever our friendship because she was served first. Her entire response was externally referented and guided by a need to manage impressions.

Our need for external referents and to manage others' impressions of us can get us into big trouble. Friendships sometimes suffer because of external referenting and impression management. One of my trainees was good friends with another trainee, whom he absolutely refused to see when his friend was being dishonest, manipulative, and controlling. His co-dependent idea of friendship was that by refusing to see these behaviors, he would see his friend only the way his friend wanted to be seen. This was a co-dependent collusion. In co-dependent relationships, we often try to help our friends be seen the way they want to be seen. We take care of each other's impression management. These friends had colluded in an effort to maintain their delusions about themselves. A good friend would notice and point out the behaviors without judgment.

One of the important things I hope I can demonstrate is how commonplace the disease of co-dependence is and how we practice it in everyday events that are taken for granted in our addictive society. A good example of co-dependence as an everyday occurrence is trying to live up to another's expectations. A lawyer whom I have used for certain specialized legal matters tried to do this with me. He had suggested that I might be able to save some tax money and promised that he would look into the details and let me know how to arrange this. Several months later, my tax consultant, financial planner, and I all became aware that we needed this information and had not yet heard from the lawyer. We called him, and he promised to put something in writing so we would understand what needed to be done. More time passed, and we still hadn't heard from my lawyer. Finally it was necessary to do my taxes without the information from the lawyer.

About a month later, he was finishing up another legal process for me. When we ran into some difficulties, I called a summit meeting and told him that my trust level was very low and that we needed to rebuild a working confidence level before we could continue. I told him that my confidence in him had begun to wane when he failed to deliver the promised tax information. He said I was absolutely right to be upset and angry, and he acknowledged that he had suggested a particular procedure and had agreed to follow up with details. He then explained that he had discovered that the procedure would not work and that he had felt terrible. He believed that he should have been able to come up with a solution, and when he could not, he did not want to have to tell me that. (I told him that this was an example of co-dependence and he would appear in my next book! He seemed pleased.) As we discussed the situation, I told him that I was not angry because he could not find a solution. I was angry because he did not inform me of this and had left all of us hanging at tax time. If there was no solution, there was no solution. Believing that you *should* have a solution is a characteristic of co-dependence.

This story is a common, everyday example of the practice of the disease. Co-dependents want to please. When they cannot, they believe they are personal failures and try to hide the fact that they cannot meet everyone's expectations. When my lawyer demonstrated that he was more concerned about pleasing me than he was about his own integrity, I became furious and he lost my trust.

Co-dependents place unrealistic expectations on themselves and when they cannot meet them, they do not understand this limitation as a fact of life; they try to manipulate and control it. Co-dependents do not know how to have clear, straight interactions. There is always much more going on than meets the eye.

Not Trusting Your Own Perceptions

Co-dependents tend to dismiss their own perceptions of situations unless and until they are verified externally by others. Even though they might have a very clear intuitive impression of a person or a situation, they will often dismiss it as crazy or "off-the-wall."

This happened recently in my presence. Three of us had occasion to meet and listen to a well-known performer. I was not impressed with his performance because he seemed depressed and lethargic. As it turned out, when he was scheduled to play again, none of the three of us wanted to attend the concert. Two of us clearly stated our perceptions, which coincided, while the third person said that she had dismissed a similar impression as crazy. Now that she realized it agreed with ours, however, she felt more like trusting it.

We see two levels of co-dependence at work here. First, she did not trust her perceptions, even though whether she was "right" or not really did not matter. They were her perceptions, and they were all she needed to make a decision about hearing the performer again. The fact that she did not trust her perceptions is characteristic of the co-dependent. (Interestingly, rigidly adhering to an opinion and not letting in any new information is also characteristic of co-dependence. Either position makes it impossible to process relevant data.)

The second level of co-dependence was the ease with which she accepted her perceptions once they were externally validated. We all could have been wrong about the performer. We were not wrong about our perceptions, however, and that is the difference. My friend will still have to work through her need for external referents in order to trust her own perceptions. Both levels are important to work through in recovery.

• Caretaking

Since co-dependents have such low self-esteem and are so externally referented, they are often caretakers. Caretaking is a special characteristic of the co-dependent, and while it naturally falls under the rubric of control, it deserves its own category for the co-dependent.

Making Yourself Indispensable

Co-dependents really doubt that anyone would want to have them around for their intrinsic worth, so they have to make themselves indispensable. One way of doing this is by "taking care of"—doing things for others that they really can and need to do for themselves.

For example, when I was more actively practicing my co-dependence, I had a good friend who was a body therapist and also an alcoholic. Since she was an excellent body therapist, I often referred clients to her. Since she was a nonrecovering alcoholic, however, she frequently failed to show up for appointments, and I would find myself confronted by an angry client. Before I started recovering from my co-dependence, I made excuses for the therapist and tried to smooth it over with the client. By doing this, I was preventing both from directly dealing with the situation, and I was putting myself in the middle (that is, making myself indispensable). As I moved into my recovery, I told my therapist friend that until she was more responsible about her work and had a better-established recovery, I did not feel free to refer new clients to her. If old clients asked about her (because she *was* good), I would tell them about her unreliability and would suggest that they handle the problem themselves. This was "caring for" myself, my friend, and my clients by dealing honestly and realistically with the situation. When we do things for others that they need to do for themselves, we are making ourselves indispensable and we are not helping them. We are "taking care of" and in so doing we facilitate another's dependence upon us.

There is no one more indispensable in an alcoholic family than the co-dependent spouse. Co-dependents need to be needed.

Being a Martyr

The prototype for the "good" co-dependent is the "good Christian" martyr (also an issue of control). Martyrs suffer, and do it gallantly. Everyone knows how much co-dependents suffer. And even their reluctance to acknowledge suffering is a way to suffer. Co-dependents believe that they are suffering for a holy cause, such as keeping the family together or hiding a spouse's drinking, and in the long run their belief in the importance of suffering just helps perpetuate a destructive situation and extend the amount of time that transpires before the persons who need help get it. Martyrs actually keep chaotic situations going by taking care of their drinkers, making excuses, making sure their households stay together, cleaning up the messes, enduring the outbursts, and so on, when blowing the whistle would have been the most caring thing to do. Since martyrs' actions look so gallant, however, it is difficult to see or experience them as symptoms of a disease.

• Physical Illness

Physical illness is also characteristic of co-dependence, which is indeed a disease that will lead to death if it is untreated. In fact, active alcoholics frequently outlive their co-dependent spouses. Frequently, I believe, co-dependents become ill from attempting to control the uncontrollable.

Co-dependents work hard. They are so intent on taking care of others, keeping things going, and surviving that they often develop stress-related functional or psychosomatic diseases.[4] They develop headaches; backaches; respiratory, heart, and gastrointestinal problems; and hypertension. Even cancer has been linked to the disease. Co-dependents also develop addictions (like eating disorders, hyperactivity, workaholism, overspending), and they sometimes even move into chemical addictions. The addictive process then moves into yet another subsyndrome.

• Self-Centeredness

The self-centeredness of co-dependents is of a different order than the self-centeredness of alcoholics, but it is no less destructive. Contrasting the two is a good example of how each subsyndrome exhibits a characteristic of the addictive process in its own peculiar fashion. The self-centeredness of co-dependents is quite subtle. In fact, co-dependents often pride themselves on being selfless (which sounds self-centered, does it not?).

By contrast, alcoholics put themselves and their drinking first. In alcoholic families, everything and everyone revolves around them and their drinking. Alcoholics are frequently openly arrogant, and they expect the world to revolve around them. In fact, the self-centeredness of alcoholics is such that they actually believe that their perspective of the universe is what defines it.

One of the most frequent forms of co-dependent self-centeredness is believing that everything that happens to a significant other happens because of something you—the co-dependent—did. Co-dependents, indeed, believe that they are the center of the universe. "Oh, you're unhappy. What did I do?" is the often-heard refrain of the co-dependent. If someone in the family is angry, co-dependents firmly believe they caused it *and* can make it better. They personalize everything! Their self-centeredness is also very intrusive: they cannot respect others enough to allow them to work out their own problems. In their self-centeredness, co-dependents are meddlers; they believe that they can and should be able to fix anything. Co-dependents take responsibility for others—their feelings, their thoughts, even their lives. This is the most gentle, loving, killing kind of self-centeredness. It is the co-dependent's brand.

This subtle kind of self-centeredness, which promotes dependence and eventually makes others resentful (most people come to hate anyone they cannot live without), is an area of great confusion for the co-dependent, and it needs to be addressed gently and with compassion in treatment. My experience in counseling has been that the co-dependent often gets the brunt of lots of unresolved hostility and anger that has built up in others, who have been controlled, smothered, manipulated, and made more dependent by the co-dependent. This anger is especially difficult for co-dependents to understand. Why should others be angry at them, when they have been trying to do all the right things? When a co-dependent is just beginning to deal with this disease, it is very difficult to see this sort of behavior as self-centered, especially when the addict's brand of self-centeredness is so clear.

I also want to point out that self-centeredness is related to lack of boundaries. Because self-centered persons place themselves at the center of the universe, everything else is defined by and through them. Hence, they do not really know where they end and others begin. They live within this dualism: I did not do anything to deserve this and I brought this on myself. The center is "I."

• Control Issues

Co-dependents are supreme controllers. They believe they can and should be able to control everything! As situations become progressively chaotic, co-dependents exert more and more control. These attempts to control are, I think, the major cause of the physical illnesses mentioned earlier.

In alcoholic families, it is easy to see how co-dependents try to control the drinking of their spouses. However, they attempt to exercise just as much control in non-alcoholic families. Co-dependents believes that they can control others' perceptions (through impression management); control how others see their families; and control what their children perceive and feel and how they will turn out. They believe that with just a little more effort, they can get their families back to normal and make things turn out the way they want. There is almost nothing that co-dependents do *not* try to control.

All of these attempts to control the uncontrollable lead to tremendous depression, because co-dependents view themselves as failures when they cannot control everything. Repeated failures cause more depression and negativity.

• Feelings

Being Out of Touch with Feelings

Co-dependents get progressively out of touch with their feelings. I suspect that people who become severe co-dependents have never been skillful at dealing with feelings, although there is no way to prove that. What I do know is that persons who are embedded in the disease of co-dependence are usually not in touch with their feelings. And when they are, the feelings tend to come out in an intense, bombastic way and be overwhelming to those around them (and often to themselves, as well).

Co-dependents have become so preoccupied in fulfilling others' expectations that they have lost touch with themselves.

They are so trained (see Chapter 5) to see others' points of view that they always put those viewpoints above their own. Co-dependents believe that when they *understand* how another feels, they have no right to have feelings of their own. In order to be accepted, they deny their own experience.

Co-dependence is a frightening state of existence. Co-dependents cannot do what they want to do because they have grown so out of touch with their feelings that they cannot determine what it is they even want.

Distorted Feelings

Since co-dependents have learned that only "acceptable" feelings can be felt, they have also learned to distort feelings. (Feelings are often distorted to maintain the impression that co-dependents want to have of themselves.) For example, if co-dependents want to see themselves as kind, loving persons and yet inwardly resent the drinking and/or the addictive behavior of their spouses, they are caught in a self-centered bind of their own making. In order to maintain that self-image, they will distort their feelings of anger into self-righteousness. Since this transformation is largely unconscious, it is just as confusing to co-dependents as it is to those around them.

Also, when feelings are repressed and distorted, resentment, anger, and depression build up and then tend to find expression in devious ways that frighten and confuse co-dependents and the persons around them. When these feelings are not dealt with through an active recovery program, jealousy and possessiveness may result. Because co-dependents have such low self-esteem, they cannot really believe that others would want to be around them unless they were forced to be there. So co-dependents try to possess other people.

Just as alcoholics use chemicals to numb their feelings, co-dependents use relationships, worrying, eating, or any number of things to avoid dealing with their feelings. While the particular form is different, the relationship to the addictive process is very similar.

• Dishonesty

For all sorts of reasons, co-dependents are involved in a process of dishonesty. To be out of touch with your feelings and unable to articulate what you feel and think is dishonest. To distrust your perceptions and therefore be unable to communicate them is dishonest. To focus on fulfilling others' expectations, whether they are right for you or not, is dishonest. Impression management is dishonest.

One of my friends just shared a story with me that is a good example of a common type of co-dependent dishonesty. The story helps illustrate the "everydayness" of this disease. This friend had not been happy with a recent haircut, so she made an appointment, at the urging of her mother and sister, with their hairdresser. Before that appointment, however, she went for a wash and set to her own hairdresser, who told her she really needed a cut. Feeling guilty, my friend developed an elaborate story about how her mother and sister had given her an appointment with another hairdresser as a gift and how she really could not turn down that gift. This sort of lying—to get yourself out of an uncomfortable spot—is characteristic of the co-dependent. We often think of it as commonplace. Unfortunately, it throws us into our disease.

The Twelve Step program teaches us that we must put our sobriety above everything else in our lives. It also teaches us that even the smallest lie can plunge us back into our disease. To preserve her sobriety, my friend needed to make amends. She had to claim her dishonesty for herself and do whatever she needed to do to make it right with her hairdresser.

Another everyday example comes from one of my trainees, who asked me to autograph a book for her. I was surprised because I thought she already had a copy of my book. She explained, however, that she had recently separated from her husband and he had taken her copy. We both agreed that it was probably a good thing, and I forgot about the conversation.

The next day, however, this woman tearfully told me that she had to make amends. Her husband had not taken the book; she had given it to him. And while that little lie did not seem like a big deal to me, she said it was affecting her greatly. She was feeling more and more uncomfortable with me and was beginning to set up a wall between us. Since she valued our friendship too much to let that happen, she needed to own her lie and make amends.

For me, one of the most challenging aspects of the disease of co-dependence is that it is so common and so ordinary. Of course, this is also one of the aspects that makes it so insidious. We know how to operate in it better than we know how not to. Ordinary as it is, co-dependence is unhealthy, however, and it will kill us, so we had better learn to recognize it and heal ourselves from it.

• Being Central

Co-dependents are suckers for the line, "You know, I have never been able to talk to anyone the way I can talk with you." Down deep, co-dependents want what they perceive to be the perfect union, which may be the same as fusion in their minds.

Co-dependents fear abandonment and need to be involved in every aspect of the lives of their significant others. It is inconceivable that a significant other would have a life without the co-dependent. Co-dependents need to be needed and have to be involved. Not to be involved in some aspect of a loved one's life is to be abandoned.

• Gullibility

Gullibility is one characteristic of co-dependence that I have rarely heard discussed and yet frequently see in co-dependents. Co-dependents tend to believe almost anything they are told, especially if it fits the way they want things to be. Gullibility, in fact, may be a form of personal and interpersonal dishonesty. The most obvious example of co-dependent gullibility is seen in the spouse of the alcoholic who continues to believe that the alcoholic will give up drinking and things will change. Long after most people would have given up, co-dependents hang in there believing things will be different.

Since they do not trust their perceptions and are not in touch with their feelings, co-dependents tend to believe what other people tell them, even if it is an obvious lie. They *want* to believe, and if they *want* it to be that way, it must be that way. (This may also be related to their control issues.) Co-dependents are notoriously bad judges of character, because they see what they want to see and hear what they want to hear.

• Loss of Morality

The dishonesty described earlier is just one form of a loss of personal morality. Lying is antithetical to us as moral beings. It is not in keeping with our deepest spiritual selves. The more enmeshed we become in our disease, the more pervasive and destructive the lying becomes. Lying to ourself is always destructive to the self, and it is always destructive to others and the self when we lie to them. This is a form of spiritual deterioration.

Another form of spiritual deterioration is the neglect of the self and the body. When we inflict unnecessary stress and bring disease upon ourselves, we lose touch with our spiritual beings.

Another especially painful form of spiritual deterioration is neglecting people we are responsible for or care a great deal about, such as our children. As we become enmeshed in our co-dependence, we neglect those we love. We may attempt to "take care of" them by trying to control them or their circumstances, yet by doing this, we do not care *for* them.

For example, I now realize that while I was spending all my energy trying to keep my household together and see that my children got what I thought they needed, I was often not really emotionally available to them when they needed me. All my energy was going into controlling the situation and seeing that the household continued to function. I was too exhausted for those "extras" that were really the essentials, like time, listening, and just being around. We become terrible parents while trying to be good parents, and we find ourselves doing things that we regret. This is spiritual deterioration, and it is a characteristic of co-dependence. You cannot recover from this disease, I believe, without reconnecting with your spirituality. (The Twelve Step program often refers to this process as a "spiritual awakening.") We are all spiritual beings, I believe, and as we move into any addictive process, we move further and further from our own spirituality. To recover, we need to return to or develop a new relationship with our spiritual selves.

• Fear, Rigidity, Judgmentalism

Much of what co-dependents do in life is motivated by fear, the basic building block of an addictive process. When people are constantly fearful, they tend to become progressively rigid in body, mind, and soul. When their universe seems overwhelming, confused, full of fearful expectations, it is not surprising that they become rigid or controlling. Co-dependents try desperately to hold on to the illusion of the world they have built, and their rigidity is an indicator that they are "into the disease."

I do not think that anyone will find it surprising that judgmentalism follows fear and rigidity. As co-dependents experience failing self-esteem, an inability to control the world, and confusion, they become progressively judgmental of others. Judgmentalism is so inherent in our system that we often fail to see it as the disease process that it is. However, when we look more closely at what it does to people who are judgmental (it leads to physical illness, alienation, unhappiness, and bitterness), it is easy to see that judgmentalism is indeed part of a disease process.

Behaviors that "Trigger" the Disease

The concept of slipping back "into the disease" or "operating out of the disease" is very useful in working with co-dependents. I want to end this chapter with a quick look at some of the behaviors that can throw co-dependents back into their disease or that indicate that they are "in" the disease after recovery has started.

When individuals first begin their recovery, their lives are so enmeshed in the disease that they do not know and/or do not remember the state of nondisease. As they work on their recovery, they begin to have brief experiences of being clear and (I think) operating out of a system that has nothing to do with the addictive system. I call the alternative a living process system, and I have come to believe that recovery, then, involves a *systems shift*. As recovery continues, co-dependents become clearer and operate more out of this other system, and they begin to have a more acute awareness of when they have slipped or are slipping back into their disease.

My trainees and I have generated a list of some one hundred behaviors that generally push recovering persons back into co-dependence and the addictive disease process. Although I am not going to list all of these behaviors here, I do want to list some so you will have a feel for these triggering mechanisms.

- The first one is dishonesty. The slightest kind of lie will usually trigger co-dependents to move away from their sobriety and back into the disease.

- Co-dependents will usually get back into the disease when they find themselves talking about others in a way that they would not be willing to talk about them in person, and when they do this to build up allies and justify themselves.

- Whenever co-dependents find themselves obsessed with a person or situation, the disease will probably be triggered.

- Whenever co-dependents become controlling and/or manipulative, the disease will probably be triggered.

- Whenever co-dependents find themselves interpreting another person and assuming they know more about that person than she/he does about her/himself, it is usually followed by a slippage back into the disease.

- Self-neglect is fertile ground for moving back into the disease.
- Comparisons are an invitation back into the disease. The process of comparing is an addictive process. Statements like "I cannot do it as well," "He is better than I am," and "If only I could be like her" are all likely to trigger the disease.
- Blaming others and/or not taking responsibility for yourself is a step toward the disease.
- Jealousy triggers the disease process.
- Dualistic thinking (thinking in poles good/bad, right/wrong, either/or) always throws co-dependents back into their disease.

These are only a few of the "triggers" that we have identified.[5] They do throw us back into the disease process. They are powerful and our awareness of their insidious power will help us live more fully in a living process system that is totally unrelated to the addictive process.

When we talk about the addictive process, we are talking about civilization as we know it.

chapter five

Co-Dependence in Its Cultural Context

Our society tends to accept the abnormal as normal when it is common. Clearly, the addictive process is common in this society, and so it is accepted as normal. But while the beliefs, behaviors, and attitudes of the addictive process may be the statistical norm for the culture (Sharon Wegscheider-Cruse says that 96 percent of the population is co-dependent), they are not necessarily "normal" for the human organism. What may be a statistical "norm" produces unnatural early death and unhappy, destructive, and destroyed persons. I do not believe that this is the "normal" state for the human organism, and I *do* believe that this disease syndrome has become the "norm" for our society.

We live in a society whose institutions are built upon and exacerbate some of the chief characteristics of the addictive process. In marriage, for example, an addictive relationship is considered normal in our culture. Most of our love songs are about addictive love and are based on its assumptions—suffering, possessiveness, cling-clung relationships, and externalizing our identity (that is, needing someone outside ourself to establish our identity). Our culture teaches our teenagers to aspire to such relationships! They are taught to want someone who cannot live without them and through whom they can find their identity; they are taught to see suffering as noble and accepted.

In this chapter, I would like to explore a few of the major characteristics of the addictive process and see how they are supported by three of our major institutions—the family, the school, and the church. Further, I will demonstrate how these institutions form us into people who will fit into an addictive system, find persons with whom we can develop co-dependent relationships, and perpetuate the system by passing its characteristics on to our offspring.

The following material is based on the *experience* of many, many affected persons as they have described it. Since I have discussed many of the characteristics of the addictive system and their expression in the disease of co-dependence in the preceding chapter, I will limit myself to four characteristics that I have not previously looked at in detail and that have obvious relevance to the family, the school, and the church: (1) frozen feelings, (2) perfectionism, (3) dishonesty, and (4) thinking disorders.

Frozen Feelings

• The Family and Feelings

One of Sharon Wegscheider-Cruse's definitions of the co-dependent is anyone who comes from an emotionally repressive family. Many of our most revered child-rearing practices are ways to help children get out of touch with their feelings and learn not to express them. We all know how frank children can be, yet much of their training teaches them how to be "nice," "polite," and "tactful." This training often leaves them unable or unwilling to express how they *really* feel or how they *really* perceive a situation. One of the "rules" of a co-dependent family (mentioned by Subby and Friel and quoted in Chapter 2) is that feelings should not be expressed openly. Children are often told that, for instance, "They don't really feel that way about Aunt Sarah," etc. Not only are they not supposed to express their feelings, they are told they do not even feel what they feel. This is really a "crazy-maker."

Many "family secrets" also lead to unexpressed feelings. Everyone in the family is aware at some level that a family secret exists, that it must never be discussed, and that any feelings about not discussing it are not to be discussed. I have also found that most families that repress feelings repress happy, positive feelings as well as feelings of anger, pain, guilt, terror, etc. *Any* feelings are suspect. Since feelings are a major source of our information about ourselves and the way we check out our perceptions of our world, repressing them sets us up to be especially vulnerable to manipulation and control.

I have a friend who comes from a family where she could not express anything but feeling "good." The main task of the children in this family was not to grow and experience their own lives, but to prove that they had a perfect family and that their parents were perfect parents. If they felt and expressed *any* other feelings, they ran the risk of destroying the family mythology. As these children became adults, they became aware of this tremendous repression and they sought to get in touch with childhood feelings. When they do this within the family, however, their parents describe them as having "problems." To express feelings is to have problems—serious problems. The perfect person is never bothered by feelings.

In many families, if the children would feel and express their feelings, the family would be forced to deal with its own reality. Not only that, if children are helped to express and explore their feelings, they lose their fear of their feelings and can find out what the feeling—whether it is sadness, fear, or joy—is about. By not allowing a full expression of feelings, our families prepare us for our addictive system.

Recovery from the addictive process requires that we experience, learn to express, and work through our feelings.

• The School and Feelings

Most of us who work with schools are painfully aware that they offer very little *affective* education. Our educational process is mostly geared towards logical, rational, linear learning, and feelings are often thought to interfere with the necessary focus upon the rational/logical.

Our educational institutions encourage us to express what we think, not what we feel. In fact, good thinking is thought to be always divorced from feelings. If we became emotional as children, we were asked to leave the room, get control of ourselves, and/or act like a big girl or boy.

In learning to respond to literature and art, for example, we are taught that it is not enough to "feel" something about a poem or piece of art. We must be able to analyze it and offer logical, rational reasons why it is good or bad. If we cannot justify, rationalize, and explain our response, it has no validity.

It is not just that our schools do not educate us to know, explore, and express our feelings, they educate us *out* of them. They prepare us to fit into a society where "frozen feelings" are the norm and the addictive process is what we are expected to live.

Here is an example out of my experience. When my son was in the fourth grade, he began to dislike his physical education class. As I talked with his principal and the P.E. teacher about this, I realized what the problem was. Because my son had been in an alternative school through the third grade, he was not aware that sports and P.E. were not supposed to be *fun*. In free school (interesting name), he played during recess and sports time and had an exuberant experience; in public school, most of the time was spent lining up, marching, and learning skills. It just was not fun and joyful. The other kids had grown up in the public school system and "knew how to act"; my son did not, so *he* was a problem. I expressed my opinion that the P.E. teacher and the school structure were the problem and that their system was preparing children to fit into a rigid and militaristic society.

That same year my son's homeroom teacher instituted what she called sharing circles in her classroom—opportunities for students to talk about their feelings. The teacher told me that my son was the only one in the room who knew how to do this and that he was a great asset and model for the others. She also stated that if a kid like this could not make it in the public schools without being destroyed, she would quit. She later did!

Our schools collude in preparing us for nonliving. They help us to learn to live with "frozen feelings."

• The Church and Feelings

The third institution I wish to explore is the church. All "sophisticated" churchgoers know that too much feeling or emotion is a threat to theology (which it probably is) and is definitely lower-class. We certainly cannot trust our own feelings, instincts, and insights to help us know and understand

God. Instead, we must rely on a belief that God can only be approached by a logical, rational brain and through a theology developed by scholars.

I hope you can see that I say this with "tongue in cheek." I don't believe this, yet I think it is very clear that the institutional church distrusts feelings and being in touch with your feelings. For example, I frequently consult with women's religious orders, and I have found that the formation process that has been used to prepare women for life in various orders was based on the suppression of feelings. The perfect nun is always happy, always caring, always pious. In order to be this way, she must ignore, suppress, and freeze her normal human emotions.

The same may be said of the "good Christian" woman, who is always sweet, caring, even-tempered, never angry, and always long-suffering. To try to fit this image is to deny our humanity and be basically dishonest. I have come to believe that "niceness" and dishonesty are inextricably bound together.

If you are alive, you have feelings, many feelings. They are a very important source of information. Not to have feelings is to fit into a society that asks us not to be fully alive.

Perfectionism

• The Family and Perfectionism

Perfectionism is another characteristic of the addictive system. In Subby and Friel's list of the rules that operate in a dysfunctional family, Rule 4 is "be strong, good, right, perfect."[1] Anything less than perfect means to fail.

When I am working with adult children of alcoholics, co-dependents, and alcoholics, I frequently hear them say things like "I was never enough," "I was never good enough," or "No matter what I did in my family or in school, it never seemed like it was enough." They believe that if they can just be perfect, they can be acceptable and accepted and things will be better.

Families tend to focus on what the children are doing wrong. Irene Kassorla, the author of a book called *Go for It,* observes that because parents love their children so much and want the very best for them, they watch them very carefully when they are little and "hover," often saying "don't do this," "don't do that," etc. She says that the goal of parents is to make their children the best people possible and, in the process, the children begin to believe that they cannot do *anything* right. Kassorla recommends reinforcing "right behavior." By emphasizing the negative, parents make their children believe they can't do anything right and foster an obsessive attachment to perfectionism, since most children want to please their parents, and if being perfect children will do it, they will try. While this theory oversimplifies some issues, it also has validity.

Perfectionism is also an issue with parents who have shaky identities themselves, see their children as extensions and reflections of themselves, and need them to justify their validity and existence. Despite the fact that these parents may love their children and want the best for them, their goal is not for Janie or Johnny to become fully Janie or Johnny. What is important is for their children to reflect well upon them and prove they are good parents. Parents who believe that they should be perfect parents, as defined by the culture, will not surprisingly transmit this belief and these parenting procedures to their children.

• The School and Perfectionism

While the schools are obvious perpetrators of perfectionism, the topic still merits some exploration. The very concept of grades assumes, of course, that perfection exists, is possible, and should be sought. The idea that perfection exists is probably the most destructive of these three assumptions. If perfection exists, it theoretically should be attainable. It is misguided assumption, however, because perfection is not a human characteristic or quality; it is a Godlike quality, as defined by the culture. Even students who do very well and make straight ''A''s are never quite perfect; they could alays have performed better. Of course, it is important to point out that these persons are never perfect *as defined externally*. In some very true sense, they are perfect the way they are, but that is not the issue. Because the system believes that perfection is possible, individuals are set up to fail.

Just imagine what an educational system would be like that gives ''A''s for being who you are in the best way you can be. Imagine what changes would occur in our educational process if we eliminated grades and competition. Try to envision a system that supports and rewards individual differences and fails no one.

Even though few talk about perfectionism in the school setting, I think it is easy to see how this concept permeates the entire structure. Interestingly enough, the unspoken ideas and assumptions of a system, because they are taken for granted, often affect us more deeply and insidiously than those that are articulted clearly. Unspoken ideas, by their nature, are not questioned and/or challenged, because they are assumed to be synonymous with reality. Perfectionism in the schools, I believe, is one of those concepts that are unspoken and taken for granted. Our children are subtly trained in our schools to adopt this character defect.

• The Church and Perfectionism

It almost seems unnecessary to write about the church and perfectionism. In the Bible we are advised to ''be ye perfect as your father in Heaven is perfect." The institutional church, I believe, has interpreted this to mean "be like God as defined by Western culture—omnipotent and omniscient." This means, as I have suggested earlier, to be rational and have no feelings other than those that are socially acceptable, Christlike, and/or Godlike.

To be perfect, as defined by the institutional church, is to be like God the controller. If you are perfect, you not only have yourself under control, you also have everything and everyone else under control. Now this makes for an impossible dilemma. Since it is not possible for us to control absolutely our own lives—much less the lives of other people—striving to do so is a prescription for failure. Yet the institutional church expects its members (and its priests and ministers) to strive for perfection. If you should be able to and cannot, then you can only be a failure. Failure is depressing, and perfectionists are depressed.

And not only does the church set up an impossible goal, it also makes itself indispensable by promising to help the individual achieve that unachievable perfection.

I prefer another interpretation of "be ye perfect," one that assumes that the way to be perfect is to be perfectly you. Doing so does not demand an external definition of perfection. Since we are human, it must involve being perfectly human, not perfectly Godlike.

Dishonesty

• The Family and Dishonesty

In my discussion of the family and frozen feelings, I pointed out how the family trains children to be out of touch with their feelings and dishonest about those feelings that are socially unacceptable. We live in a society where dishonesty is a norm, and the family trains us well to fit into that society.

I had a friend who was an incest victim. In fact, it appeared that several of the children in her family were incest victims. No one talked about it, however; it was a family secret. Because of this secret, the family had become progressively dishonest. The parents were so fearful this issue might come up that communication in the family became tightly constricted. Eventually, so few topics were open to discussion that conversations in the family became dull and boring (not to mention tense and controlled). It was not until several of the "children"—as adults—went into therapy and began examining some of their personal issues that they found their voices and began to talk to one another again. This is an example of training in dishonesty. The children learned that there are some things you just cannot say.

I knew another family, with two teenage daughters, that practiced another form of dishonesty. I once called to speak with one of the daughters, who told me in the course of our conversation that her parents were out of town. I asked where they were, and she did not know, which seemed rather strange to me, since the parents apparently planned to be gone for several days. When I asked her why her parents were away (always being a curious sort), the daughter told me that her mother was being interviewed for a job as a college president and that both parents had gone for the interview. I was thrilled, offered congratulations, and asked the name of the school. Again the daughter did not know, because the parents did not talk with the "children" (they were seniors in high school!) about such matters. Even though everyone in that family would be affected by a move, the parents kept their comings and goings hidden from the rest of the family. This too is a form of family dishonesty.

• The School and Dishonesty

Schools also train our children in dishonesty. One way they do this is by homogenizing the learning process. The educational system assumes that everyone learns in essentially the same way (visually, rather than tactilely or kinesthetically) and at the same rate. Individuals are to adapt their styles and rates to those of the class and the instructor. This process in and of itself can promote dishonesty.

I referred earlier to my son's difficulties in gym class. Part of the problem was that he was offended by how the P.E. teacher treated the students, including him. When I raised this problem with the principal, he said, "Well, maybe the gym teacher was in the wrong, but couldn't you just instruct your son to go along with him and bring up his arguments later?" I said no, that teaching dishonesty for the sake of convenience helps contribute to later dishonesties, maybe even tragedies like the massacre at Mai Lai. I did not want my son to participate in a Mai Lai and then question it later. This principal was asking for what perhaps is the worst dishonesty—dishonesty with the self, from which all other dishonesties stem.

Another example comes out of my experience working in a school system, where one of the white students, whose father was a teacher at the school, became involved with one of the black students, an outstanding athlete. Although the students were from different social classes and races, their relationship was important to them. While both sets of parents were upset, they were also willing to let the relationship run its course.

I had occasion to talk with both students, both parents, and all the others involved. During one conversation with the young man, I learned that he had recently and suddenly told the young woman that he could not see her anymore.

At first, he would not explain why. I investigated and discovered that the principal had warned the young man that he would undermine all his chances for a college scholarship if he persisted in this relationship. He also threatened him with expulsion if he reported these threats to anyone. The young man was terrified and withdrew from the relationship. No one on the faculty or the staff was willing to admit how the principal's behavior ultimately threatened their lives and jobs. They all acted as if nothing had happened. They were all participating in a lie.

I have worked with enough school systems to know that those in authority frequently step over their legal and moral limits, just as this principal did. Students recognize this kind of dishonesty, resent it, and see it modeled by adults in the educational system.

I heard about still another example of personal dishonesty in the schools in a recent workshop, where a woman related an early experience of what she now calls "betrayal" in her life. When she was a child, the kids in her class played pranks on the teacher—the usual tacks on the seat, rubber snakes, etc. They also whistled when the teacher turned her back on the class, and when she demanded to know who the whistlers were, no one responded. One day the teacher had a long talk with the class and announced that if the students doing the whistling would admit it, they would not be punished. The next day, the woman in my workshop happened to whistle in class and when the teacher asked who was responsible, she held up her hand. The teacher then grabbed her, pulled her to the front of the classroom, and said that if she wanted to whistle so badly, she could just stand in front of the others and whistle for a while—treatment she definitely experienced as punishment, despite the teacher's promise that there would be no recriminations. On the following day, someone else in her part of the room whistled and the teacher asked if she had done it; she said no, but was again grabbed, shaken badly, and called a liar. Not only had this woman been lied to, she had also been taught that honesty did not pay. Years after the event, she still carries this incident with her and calls it an early experience of "betrayal."

Another example of systemic dishonesty involves what is demanded of gays who work for the school system. In many places, gays are forced to lie about who they are as persons in order to keep their jobs. The students see this systemic dishonesty and the result is frequently an increasing disrespect for the school system.

When students hear about the value of honesty and yet see their faculty and administration being dishonest in the ways I have mentioned, they experience the actions as speaking louder than the words. The *process* learning that occurs in our schools is frequently more powerful than the *content* learning, and what students seem to devote the most time to is learning how to beat the system. So much energy is spent on that learning that little is left for content. And since much of this process learning goes unspoken, it enters the realm of dishonesty. When we do not articulate the obvious and underlying assumptions of a system, they become the source of unspoken power.

One of the main duties of the school is to prepare young people to fit into a society that is based upon dishonesty. As long as this goal is unarticulated, it will continue. This process learning will be more powerful than any subject the school will teach. The dishonesty of co-dependents is not to know what they need, to be externally referented, to be looking outside themselves for their value. The school certainly teaches all of this.

• The Church and Dishonesty

The dishonesty in the church is perhaps the most devastating institutionalization of dishonesty in our society, because it takes place within the realm of the spirit—the very essence of our being. To teach dishonesty here is to threaten our very core.

The church teaches so many forms of dishonesty that I find it difficult to know where to start. I think it best to start with the personal and move to the institutional.

The following examples come from the personal experiences of persons in workshops I conduct. These are not people who are out to "get the church," by the way. They are persons of great faith and spirituality, who truly wanted to be able to trust the church and were devastated by their experiences.

One woman told of having an older brother who had been born with cerebral palsy. When she came along three years later, he had not developed normal motor and verbal skills, so in many ways she became his teacher and took on the burden of helping him learn to walk. Unfortunately, he simply did not have the motor skills necessary, and she met with great pain and frustration. One day in her school, however, she was told by a nun that if she were pure and prayed for something, she would get it. That night, with the sincerity only a child can muster, the girl prayed and prayed that her brother would be able to walk. The next morning, she jumped out of her top bunk and pulled him quickly out of his bed. He collapsed on the floor. Her faith, which had been tremendously strong, was badly shaken. Of course, she had the option of making herself "wrong" and believing that she was just not "pure" enough (a good loophole). In fact, what she *experienced* was being lied to.

Another short example is worth relating. At one of my workshops, another woman, who has a very deep spirituality and has had to work for it, reported her experience of the church lying to her. She had been told that God was Lutheran—Missouri Synod to be exact—and warned that if she spent time with others who did not know and/or believe this, her faith would be destroyed.

There are several levels of dishonesty here. The obvious one is that no one owns God. Second, and maybe more importantly, is the discrepancy between what her particular church taught and faith. She may shed her brainwashing if she is exposed to others, *and* her brainwashing may or may not have anything to do with faith.

One obvious dishonesty taught by the church concerns "niceness." I am not talking about caring, or loving, or goodness; I am talking about being "nice." I have found that the people who are often the nicest are those who are most out of touch with their own feelings. They are nice on the outside, but often have covered up many repressed and/or unexperienced feelings and are seething underneath. In order to be what the church says we should be, it is frequently necessary to deny who we are. No one is always nice. No one is always even-tempered. No one is always willing to be at another's disposal. No one is always willing to sacrifice herself or himself for others. The co-dependent is, however, and co-dependence is considered a disease. In training us to be "nice," the church actively trains us to be co-dependents.

The genesis of niceness is interesting. It stems from accepting an external referent of who and what we should be. The characteristics of the "good Christian" person may or may not have anything to do with who an individual really is, for example. Instead, "niceness" is determined, abstractly, to be a virtue. Who a person is remains completely irrelevant. Once the church and society have determined who the "good" person is, then individuals need to mold themselves to fit that description as closely as possible. This process is terribly dishonest and disrespectful, because it assumes that people are not acceptable the way they are and that something artificial like "niceness" has to be imposed upon them.

As we know, much incest and battering goes on in Christian families that often maintain the image of the perfect family. I wonder how the absolution of the confessional actually perpetuates these behaviors and makes dishonesty possible. Does the opportunity to confess and be absolved, in essence, perpetuate the behavior?

The dishonesty of the church is at least as impressive on the institutional level. Some years ago, I was asked to consult on a special project for a national church. The members of the group I met with had been working on the project and asked me to evaluate their work so far. When I reviewed the design of the project, I was quite startled. Not only did it *not* do what was asked, I felt that its recommendations could possibly be physically and psychologically dangerous in the hands of untrained leaders. In my usual fashion, I asked those who had contracted with me if they really wanted my input. They assured me that they did, so I gave it to them, and I later learned that many committee members agreed with my evaluation completely and, in fact, had never been happy with the project.

Despite my evaluation, however, the group decided to go ahead with the project against my and their better judgments, knowing that it could be dangerous. The reason: because of the time and money spent so far, the group didn't want to abandon the project and lose credibility. This is dishonesty at the institutional level.

You might want to give some thought to the following kinds of dishonesty we find in the institutional church. What about an international church that is opposed to birth control and holds stock in companies that manufacture birth control pills? What about churches that actively recruit all races, sexes, and kinds of people into the fold and then bar them from positions of power and decision making? This, I believe, is institutional dishonesty, and the church is deeply involved in it.

When our major formative institutions train us in dishonesty and participate in it, it is not surprising that so many people are confused about what personal honesty is. Dishonesty, one of the major character defects of co-dependents, is obviously not something they invent on their own.

Thinking Disorders

• The Family and Thinking Disorders

When children grow up in a dishonest, confused family system, their major survival mechanism is to try to figure out what is going on and then control it. In this kind of family system, you learn to think obsessively.

When professionals use the term *thinking disorder* in the clinical field, they are usually referring to a serious psychological disorder, such as schizophrenia. I am using the term in a much broader sense. I believe that the kind of confused, obsessive thinking that we see in the alcoholic (which A.A. calls "stinkin' thinkin'") and in the co-dependent is on the same continuum with the kind of thinking that we see in a greater degree and with more intensity in the schizophrenic. I also believe that this kind of thinking disorder is supported by our families, our schools, and our churches.

Confused thinking evolves out of confused situations. When dishonesty in families is the norm, there is confusion about what is really happening, who said what, what is real, etc. In the face of this kind of confusion, the human brain tries to make sense of its situation and "figure it out." As we see in recovery, "figuring it out" is a subtle attempt at control and is almost always ineffective. There is a strong belief that if I can just figure things out, everything will be all right, and I will be all right. Figuring things out almost always involves both obsessive thinking patterns and a kind of grandiosity—the belief that it is possible to make sense out of confusion, even when confusion is the norm.

• The School and Thinking Disorders

It should not come as a surprise to you if I point out that schools focus almost exclusively on logical, rational, objective, and analytic thinking. I believe that this kind of thinking—when it is not balanced by the wise, intuitive, and feeling components of the right brain, the brain stem, the body, and the being—is essentially useless and contributes to the basic illness of the society.

What A.A. calls "stinkin' thinkin' " is analytic, obsessive thinking, the constant attempt to "figure things out." Our educational institutions teach us to remove ourselves from ourselves and that which we study, make ourselves and others "objects," and then analyze both. Don't think that I place no value on this kind of thinking process. Analysis is and can be fun. I love to work with mathematical equations and analyze problems in physics or the social sciences, and I love to think about a problem and try to solve it. It's like a game. When that game becomes reality, however, when I believe that being obsessed with a problem can solve it, then I am in trouble.

The daughter of a good friend was recently killed in a horrible, senseless automobile accident. No matter how obsessive we became about the details, we could not change the reality. And no matter how many details we might have concerned ourselves with prior to the accident, we could not have prevented it. Our analysis and obsessive thinking really did not help and are not as powerful as our institutions would lead us to believe.

Our schools simply do not train us in intuitive, non-rational, nonlinear thinking. They do not train us to synthesize the data of our lives. They do not train us to utilize all our sources of information, particularly our feelings. Moreover, they teach us that when we cannot figure out a problem, we have failed. Our brains cannot control our universe and yet we are led to believe that they can. This belief can make us obsessive.

• The Church and Thinking Disorders

The relationship of the church to the kind of thinking disorder that is inherent in the disease of co-dependence is much more subtle to describe. It may be best described as a lack of faith. Basically, the church teaches us that we can control our life and our destiny by doing the right things and by being the right kind of person. This, of course, is a fallacy, since we do not control our lives. We can *influence* our lives; we cannot control them. Thinking that is based on control leads straight to the addictive process and the disease of co-dependence. When we put ourselves in the driver's seat or play God, we become enmeshed in the addictive system.

The basic theological process is a good example of what I mean by "stinkin' thinkin'." It is fascinating to watch scholars try to prove God's existence logically and approach the process of God solely with the left brain. We are taught to think about God in this left-brain way, and the more sophisticated we become, the more circular our thinking becomes. Unfortunately, this method misses an important element of spirituality, and it trains our spirituality to fit into our addictive society.

This system trains us to devalue ourselves, be dishonest, detach ourselves from our feelings, and referent ourselves externally in order to become good co-dependents.

•   •

The four characteristics of the addictive process and co-dependence that I have discussed in this chapter do not exhaust the possibilities. In fact, they are only a few of the characteristics named in Chapter 4. I wanted to demonstrate, however, how the family, the school, and the church collude in developing and perpetuating this illness. We have to understand the systemic nature of the disease in order to see it in its proper context.

To be a living process therapist is to embrace a whole new way of being in the world.

chapter six

Treatment and Co-Dependence

My experience with the treatment of co-dependence comes from several sources: the experience of going through family treatment myself; hearing about the experiences of clients, trainees, and friends who have gone through family programs; and my experience as a consultant to treatment programs.

As a result of this experience, I've become aware of some glaring problems and oversights within treatment programs that could be modified to make the programs stronger. I want to focus on some of those changes and then discuss treatment approaches that I have been developing over the past few years and that have proven very successful. While I have had good treatment experiences and believe that I and others have been helped, I have some general concerns about treatment and would like to voice those concerns and suggest some lways to correct the problems I see. My major interest, at this point, is in training treatment staffs and consulting with them as they work with co-dependents.

Treatment of Co-Dependence in the Past and Present

• **Referented to the Addict**

As I have suggested earlier, the treatment of co-dependence came into being as an adjunct to the treatment of the alcoholic; the family was often brought into treatment to support (or at least not undermine) the recovery of the alcoholic. Historically, co-dependents were used to either confront or support the alcoholic. Either way, the focus was on the alcoholic.

Early on in CD treatment, no one recognized that co-dependents needed specific treatment programs designed for their particular needs. There was little or no recognition that the alcoholic and the co-alcoholic were struggling with some of the same issues and some very different issues and needed to be treated in similar *and* dissimilar ways.

My experience has been that almost all of the information presented during the conventional treatment process concerned the disease of alcoholism. Family members would leave those week-long sessions knowing a great deal about alcoholism and very little about their own disease and what to do with it.

• **Nonrecovering Co-Dependents**

Many of these earlier treatment programs were in fact quite hostile, in a subtle way, towards the co-dependent. The programs were often conducted by persons who were recovering alcoholics and *nonrecovering* co-dependents themselves. This led to several interesting dynamics. First, the person directing the treatment program would identify with the alcoholic, not with the co-dependent. In a chemical dependency treatment model, the most significant words are,

"I know how you feel because I am recovering from the same disease." A lack of identification between the counselor and the co-dependent inhibits the co-dependent's recovery, is a great limitation, and complies more with a mental health model than it does with a CD model.

Second, the treatment program was often conducted by persons who had significant unresolved issues with the co-dependents in their own lives. Since they were not recognizing and actively working with their own co-dependence, the spouses and families of the alcoholic got some of the fallout from the counselor's unresolved issues. For example, my extended family and I set up a co-dependence treatment program for ourselves that was conducted by the director of a family treatment center. During our treatment, we were constantly told that we were sicker than the alcoholic. I pointed out that such a statement felt hostile and irrelevant. We were admitting that we were sick by setting up a treatment program for ourselves, and we were there to work on our recovery. Continually hearing that we were "sicker" than the alcoholic did not facilitate anything useful. What I now recognize is that making comparisons ("you are *sicker*") is a characteristic of codependence. We were being confronted with our counselor's unresolved issues.

This brings us to a third dynamic: counselors are often, themselves, untreated co-dependents and this means, I believe, that the actual treatment process often hooks into their unresolved disease and triggers co-dependence issues for those counselors. It is hard enough for persons with well-established sobriety from their co-dependence to avoid getting hooked by the disease. For those who do not have well-established sobriety, it is almost impossible!

We are recognizing increasingly that people in the "helping" professions tend to be nonrecovering co-dependents and that people who work with recovering alcoholics tend to become co-dependents in relation to the people with whom they work. We have not recognized fully, however, what this means in the treatment of the co-dependent. We need to examine how much the treatment of co-dependence involves the practice of the disease by the counselor.

- ## Characteristics of the Disease in Treatment

- *External referent.* As I have described in detail, a major characteristic of co-dependence is being externally referented. When treatment focuses solely on the alcoholic and the needs of the alcoholic, co-dependence is perpetuated.

- *Comparison.* The disease is built on comparison and competition. When comparisons are used in the treatment process itself, they perpetuate the disease.

- *Controlling.* A major characteristic of the disease is controlling behavior. When control is modeled by the counselor, the disease is actively present. For example, I have seen many counselors tell their clients that they must get in touch with their feelings in order to get well. When the clients finally begin to articulate their feelings, however, the counselor moves into a controlling mode and either begins to talk, changes the focus, or touches the client, thus keeping the expression of feelings under the counselor's control.

- *Answers.* Co-dependents feel that part of their role in life is to find answers and explain things for others. Interpretation is the practice of the disease of co-dependence. To recover, they need to do the hard work of finding their own answers, and they need to have this modeled in their recovery programs. Interpreting and believing that you should have answers for others *is* the disease itself.

These are some of the problems I see occurring in the treatment of co-dependence at present. I will discuss some other relevant issues in Chapter 7.

Treatment of Co-Dependence in the Mental Health Field

• Nonrecognition of the Problem

The first and foremost issue that must be faced is that mental health practitioners do not recognize co-dependence and link it to addictions. The mental health field has simply not identified the addictive process and the syndrome of co-dependence because people in the field are nonrecovering co-dependents who have not recognized that their professional practice is closely linked with the practice of their untreated disease. Moreover, the mental health theories and conceptualizations regarding treatment have often come directly out of the active practice both of the unrecognized disease of the addictive process and its subdiseases of chemical addiction and co-dependence. Recent findings, for instance, indicate that Freud was probably an untreated drug addict, which means that his theories evolved at least partially out of the kind of thinking, perceptions, and assumptions found in the chemically dependent (e.g., "stinkin' thinkin' "; dualism; and obsessive logical, rational thinking), which differ from normal thinking patterns.

• Controlling

Traditional psychotherapies have controlled clients. The therapist is presumed to be "in charge," to know what is best for the client, and to act on that knowledge. This is the disease of co-dependence. The medical model comes out of a co-dependent model.

• Fragmentation

One way to perpetuate the disease is to refuse to see the whole and to focus on smaller parts, which provides the illusion of doing something while you ignore the real issue. For example, when you work with narcissism as an issue and fail to see that it is also the self-centeredness of the addictive process, the treatment gets somewhat skewed.

• Intellectual/Cognitive Focus

I do not believe that recovery from co-dependence is possible when the therapist works only on a cognitive level. You have to lead with the feelings and inner process, and *then* bring the treatment to the cognitive level, not the other way around. Practitioners of traditional mental health techniques do not know how to do that.

• Spirituality

Recovery from the disease of co-dependence is impossible without recognizing and working with spiritual issues as healing issues. Mental health practitioners do not know how to do that. In fact, in mental health circles, there is great suspicion of the spiritual. The mental health field has confused spirituality and religion and does not know what to do with either.[1]

New Treatment Models and Treatment Issues to Be Addressed

• Need to Treat the Paradox

Co-dependence is both a generic/systemic disease and a specific disease. Both forms need to be treated actively for treatment to be successful. Hence, co-dependents need to learn about the addictive process and the specifics of co-dependence. A both/and approach is necessary.

• Co-Dependents Need to Be with Other Co-Dependents

Just as an alcoholic is helped by the insights and support of other alcoholics, so also the co-dependent needs the insight and support of other co-dependents. Much of the treatment and learning can and should come from one another. We simply cannot underestimate the healing effects of being with other persons who are struggling with the same problems.

• The Treatment Staff

The staff that treats co-dependents needs to be made up of primary co-dependents who have established a good sobriety from their co-dependence and who themselves acknowledge and are actively recovering from the disease. (They can say, "I know how you feel.") Staff members need to recognize that working in this field is a constant invitation to indulge in their disease, and they need the tools and support to continue focusing on their own recovery as well as the recovery of the client. If staff members do not admit that they are actively recovering, they become part of the problem and impede the progress of the client.

• Cognitive Treatment Is Not Adequate

Cognitive treatment alone is not adequate for the recovery of the co-dependent. To deal only with the analytical, rational, and logical is to perpetuate the disease. Some authors—Janet Woititz, Sondra Smalley, and Sharon Wegscheider-Cruse, to mention a few—have worked on the etiology of co-dependence. What they are learning is interesting and helpful. Sometimes, however, I feel that the greatest use for this knowledge is to make the professional feel secure in having it. If it prevents the counselor from dealing with the client on a feeling and/or process level, it can harm and interfere with treatment. We can see that it is interesting to speculate, as Smalley and others in the field have done, that co-dependence is related to a shame-based childhood. However, if this intellectualization or left-brain activity keeps an individual from coming to this understanding in her or his own process way, it can be counterproductive to recovery, and it can even serve to keep that person operating within the disease.

To recover, co-dependents need to explore and experience their own deep process in a noncognitive way.

• Family Treatment Model

A family treatment model, such as family reconstruction, is both useful and inadequate in and of itself for recovery. Since only one aspect of the disease of co-dependence is that it is a family disease, treatment of the family should only be one part of the program of recovery. Co-dependence is also an individual disease and has to be treated as such. Understanding and working with the family system dynamics is helpful; ultimately, however, individuals have to take responsibility for (not blame) and claim their own lives. Too much focus upon the family system may possibly rob individuals of their personal process and the recovery inherent in that process.

• The System

Co-dependents need to understand what the addictive system is and how their particular disease of co-dependence is related to this system. This approach is also necessary for understanding the concept of a systems shift and where such a shift fits into treatment.

• The Twelve Step Program

I believe that the Twelve Step program is a crucial tool for recovering co-dependents and one of the best tools for making a systems shift. From my perspective, recovery from co-dependence (and other addictive processes!) means leaving the addictive system and moving into a living process system, which, I believe, is the normal, healthy system for the human organism.

• Living Process Therapy

For the last fifteen years or so, I have been developing an approach to therapy that I call *living process therapy*. In some ways, this is an inadequate term because the word *process* is used in so many different ways by so many different people. Many say that they work with processes and do process therapy, even though their work is nothing like mine. Unfortunately, some of what is called process therapy continues to operate out of the assumptions of the addictive system. I often say to my trainees that to be a living process therapist is to embrace a whole new way of being in the world. As we make a systems shift ourselves, we work differently with people. I have been training people (mostly other therapists) in living process therapy for several years, and the major focus of that training is helping them come to terms with the addictive system and co-dependence by working with their own process to make a systems shift.

I believe that living process therapy bypasses the cognitive and works with other parts of the brain and the being and then brings it back to the cognitive for closure. I also believe this is where real healing (not just adjustment) occurs.

• Combinations

For the co-dependent, I think that a combination of the models described above constitutes the most powerful treatment program. Like alcoholism, co-dependence is a cunning and baffling disease. It is also a disease for which recovery is guaranteed if you work at recovery and are willing and able to make a systems shift. This is also true for all the syndromes of the addictive process. Healing takes support, good tools (those listed here), and hard work. All three are available to us.

I have found that a combination of living process therapy and the Twelve Step program is the most effective tool for working with the co-dependent. In the hands of a skilled process facilitator, who has a personal understanding of the Twelve Step program, treatment progresses rapidly.

To avoid perpetuating the addictive process,
we must develop new approaches to theorizing
and new theories that more accurately fit our
experience and knowledge.

chapter seven

Implications

We have been looking at some rather unusual and, I think, exciting ideas about the disease of co-dependence, how theories and constructs are developed from various approaches, and how co-dependence relates to the addictive process system and a shift to a living process system. I believe that the concept of co-dependence does, indeed, have the possibility of offering entirely new ways of thinking about healthy and fully functioning individuals.

In order for this sort of systems shift to happen, however, we must make some major changes in the ways we think about and perceive the world. We must use the knowledge of the chemical dependency field, the women's and men's movement, family therapy, spirituality, and mental health to develop new models. We need to develop models that are not, in themselves, a continuation of the addictive system and its processes. To avoid perpetuating the addictive process, we must develop new approaches to theorizing and new theories that more accurately fit our experience and knowledge.

As I have said earlier, I have some grave concerns about the political issues that are emerging in this area (such as control, competition, and what treatment approaches will prevail in the field) because of the growing awareness that treating addicts and co-dependents is lucrative and prestigious. Until fairly recently, most treatment centers were staffed by people who, themselves, were recovering persons. Because many of these people do not have advanced degrees (they often have certificates in chemical dependency counseling), they are usually at or near the bottom of the financial, power, and prestige barrel when they work in the traditional medical and/or mental health settings. In order to become "acceptable" and to increase their status and earning power, they have to enter into "traditional" mental health or medical tracks by going back to school and getting degrees in counseling, social work, nursing, or psychology. This concerns me, since I believe that traditional training may, in fact, make these persons less proficient in their work with addicts and co-dependents, since the theory and practice they learn in traditional institutions comes out of addictive thinking patterns. (Most physicians and psychiatrists who become really well-versed in chemical dependency theory and treatment are themselves recovering persons.) I am also concerned that, because of the political clout held by traditional medical and mental health professionals, the chemical dependency approaches to treating co-dependence are coming under their control.

Another group of professionals bears mentioning here: persons who were trained in the traditional mental health field and were subsequently forced to confront their own addictions and/or co-dependence. They have faced the demons of their own addictive processes, and are coming out on the other side. These people (social workers, psychologists, ministers, physicians, psychiatrists, and counselors) are a breed apart. They recognize that some of the characteristics of the traditional mental health field—denial, control, and dishonesty, to name a few—actually threaten their own personal sobriety. They are involved in Twelve Step programs, share their spiritual concerns in healing, and have a completely different approach to co-dependence than the mental health establishment. These persons, I believe, form a very significant group. They have been trained and have clout in the mental health field, and they are also working out of a theory and employing practices developed from their own experiential involvement in the disease.

Right now, most of these people are working in treatment centers in the chemical dependency field, and they have had an important impact on that field. Unfortunately, because they are in the CD field, they are making little or no impact on the mental health field at large—yet. I think they can and will. Quite possibly, they will become the source to which the mental health field will turn to help heal individuals and the culture as a whole.

If we believe that a large percentage of the population—professional and nonprofessional—is in some way involved in this disease, then it is a major issue. If the traditional theories are outgrowths of this disease, then we need some major paradigm shifts.

In fact, we are already making major paradigm shifts, and I believe that the concept of co-dependence is an important vehicle for this. Such a concept promises to have significant implications politically, financially, theoretically, and personally. The times can be exciting if we do not practice the rigidity of our disease by resisting new ideas and approaches. I believe we are ready for major changes. Let's make them happen.

Notes

Introduction

1. For clarity across various professional fields, I have decided to use the term *co-dependence* instead of *co-dependency* throughout.
2. Robert Subby, "Inside the Chemically Dependent Marriage: Denial & Manipulation," in *Co-Dependency: An Emerging Issue* (Pompano Beach, Fla.: Health Communications, 1984), 29.

Chapter 1: History and Development

1. Charles Whitfield, "Co-Dependency: An Emerging Problem Among Professionals," in *Co-Dependency: An Emerging Issue* (Pompano Beach, Fla.: Health Communications, 1984), 51.
2. I have attempted to do this in my previous book, *Women's Reality* (Minneapolis: Winston Press, 1981).

Chapter 2: Definitions

1. Sharon Wegscheider-Cruse, "Co-Dependency: The Therapeutic Void," in *Co-Dependency: An Emerging Issue* (Pompano Beach, Fla.: Health Communications, 1984), 1.
2. Subby, 26.
3. Subby, 26.
4. Subby, 27.
5. Robert Subby and John Friel, "Co-Dependency: A Paradoxical Dependency," in *Co-Dependency: An Emerging Issue* (Pompano Beach, Fla.: Health Communications, 1984), 32.
6. Subby and Friel, 33.
7. Whitfield, "Co-Dependency: An Emerging Problem Among Professionals," 45.
8. Earnie Larsen, *Basics of Co-Dependency* (Brooklyn Park, Minn.: E. Larsen Enterprises, 1983).

Chapter 3: A Disease Within the Addictive Process

1. The Twelve Steps are reprinted with the permission of Alcoholics Anonymous World Services, Inc.
2. Whitfield, "Co-Dependency: An Emerging Problem Among Professionals," 50–51.

3. Kathy Cappell-Sowder, "On Being Addicted to the Addict: Co-Dependent Relationships," in *Co-Dependency: An Emerging Issue* (Pompano Beach, Fla.: Health Communications, 1984), 20.

Chapter 4: Characteristics of Co-Dependence

1. The addictive system is the subject of another book I am currently working on.
2. Masanobu Fukuoka, *The One Straw Revolution* (New York: Bantam, 1985).
3. Sharon Wegscheider-Cruse, *Co-Dependency* (St. Paul, Minn.: Nurturing Networks, Inc., 1984), 3–4.
4. Charles Whitfield, "Co-Alcoholism: Recognizing a Treatable Illness," *Family and Community Health* 7 (Summer 1984).
5. Others have described similar characteristics or behaviors that may result in or be a part of the relapse process. See Terence T. Gorski and Merlene Miller, *Counseling for Relapse Prevention* (Independence, Mo.: Herald House, 1982).

Chapter 5: Cultural Context

1. Subby and Friel, 38.

Chapter 6: Treatment

1. Charles Whitfield has a new book on this subject, *Alcoholism, Other Drug Problems, Other Attachments, and Spirituality: Stress Management and Serenity during Recovery* (Baltimore: The Resource Group, 1985).

Resources

Black, Claudia. *It Will Never Happen to Me!* Denver: M.A.C., 1981.

_____ . *Repeat After Me*. Denver: M.A.C., 1985.

Co-Dependency: An Emerging Issue. Pompano Beach, Fla.: Health Communications, 1984.

Schaef, Anne Wilson. *Women's Reality: An Emerging Female System in a White Male Society*. Minneapolis: Winston Press, 1981, 1985.

Wegscheider, Sharon. *Another Chance: Hope and Health for the Alcoholic Family*. Palo Alto, Calif.: Science and Behavior Books, 1981.

Wegscheider-Cruse, Sharon. *Choicemaking: For Co-Dependents, Adult Children and Spirituality Seekers*. Pompano Beach, Fla.: Health Communications, 1985.

Whitfield, Charles. *Alcoholism, Other Drug Problems, Other Attachments, and Spirituality: Stress Management and Serenity during Recovery*. Baltimore: The Resource Group, 1985.